COMPANION

W9-AVC-776

U.S. COINS
& CURRENCY
3rd Edition

Arlyn G. Sieber

Published by

Krause Publications, a division of F+W Media, Inc.
700 East State Street • Iola, WI 54990-0001
715-445-2214 • 888-457-2873
www.krausebooks.com

Based on the original work by Allen G. Berman

To order books or other products call toll-free 1-800-258-0929
or visit us online at www.shopnumismaster.com

ISBN-13: 978-1-4402-3089-9
ISBN-10: 1-4402-3089-7

Designed by Jana Tappa
Edited by Arlyn Sieber

Printed in China

Dedicated to all collectors for

their role in preserving history.

Contents

Preface

A number of important additions and revisions have been made to this third edition of *U.S. Coins & Currency* in the Warman's Companion series. Foremost among them is the addition of composition specifications for gold and silver coins.

Volatility in the gold and silver bullion markets has dominated recent market activity for collectible gold and silver coins. Precious metal content provides the base value for any gold or silver coin. For example, silver dollars traditionally contain 0.76 troy ounces of silver. So if silver is selling for $30 a troy ounce, any silver dollar is worth at least $22.80 (30 x 0.76).

Gold and silver coins with collectible or numismatic value sell for a premium above their precious metal value. The extent of the premium depends on the coin's grade, its rarity, and the demand for the coin in the collectibles market. Premiums over precious metal content can vary from a few percentage points for bullion coins to several hundred percent for high-quality or rare collectible coins. If the premium is high, the coin is not affected as much by fluctuating market prices for silver and gold bullion. If the premium is low, the coin's value is more likely to be affected by the ups and downs of the bullion markets.

The addition of composition information – specifically, how much precious metal a coin contains – will help readers of *U.S. Coins & Currency* track the current base value of gold and silver coins in a volatile precious metals market. A number of websites and financial news services publish current gold and silver prices. Precious metals prices also are published in many daily newspapers.

All coin and paper money values in this third edition of *U.S. Coins & Currency* have been reviewed and updated. New issues released since the last edition was published have also been added. The year 2009 saw the release of 1 cent coins with special reverses marking the bicentennial of Abraham Lincoln's birth. The same year also saw the release of quarters with reverses commemorating the District of Columbia and other U.S. territories. The year 2010 saw the kickoff of the U.S. Mint's America the Beautiful quarters series, which will honor national parks and other national sites. The series is scheduled to run through 2021.

Also in 2009, the Mint began issuing the Sacagawea dollar coin with a different reverse each year to honor the contributions of Indian tribes and individual Native Americans to the country's development and history. In addition, the Mint continues its series of Presidential dollars introduced in 2007 and the companion First Spouse gold $10 coins introduced the same year.

The paper money listings also have been updated to include new series issued since the last edition of *U.S. Coins & Currency* was published and technological advances in the production of U.S. paper money.

Coins introduction

The decimal system of coinage used in the United States today is based largely on a proposal put forth by Thomas Jefferson in the nation's fledgling years. Coinage was scarce in Colonial America. The mother country, Great Britain, held on tightly to its royal right to mint coins. The few coins that did circulate in the Colonies were foreign issues brought to America by trade with other countries or settlers arriving from other lands. Thus, barter largely fueled commerce in the Colonies.

Upon establishment of the United States, the Articles of Confederation originally granted individual states the right to produce copper coins. These state issues, along with foreign coins, circulated during the country's early days, but the mishmash of state-issued and foreign coins and their varying standards was unwieldy and susceptible to fraud and counterfeiting, particularly in interstate commerce.

In 1782, U.S. Superintendent of Finance Robert Morris proposed establishing a national mint that could produce a standard coinage for use throughout the country. Despite approval from a congressional committee, Morris was unable to follow through on his plan, and Thomas Jefferson picked up the cause in 1784. But again, the effort got bogged down in debate over various proposals for a national coinage.

Finally, in April 1792, Congress passed an act establishing the U.S. Mint. The act authorized the following denominations: half cent and cent in copper; "half disme," "disme," quarter dollar, half dollar, and dollar in silver; and a quarter eagle ($2.50), half eagle ($5), and eagle ($10) in gold. The denominations and standards were based largely on Jefferson's proposal for a decimal coinage. "The most easy ratio of multiplication and division is that by ten," Jefferson wrote. "Every one knows the facility of Decimal Arithmetic."

1792 half disme.

The following July, the Mint produced 1,500 silver half dismes, or 5-cent pieces, which are regarded as the nation's first official coinage. U.S. coinage began in earnest in 1793 with the production of more than 35,000 half cents and more than 36,000 cents. By 1796, in addition to half cents and cents, the Mint was producing silver half dimes, dimes, quarters, half dollars, and dollars, and gold $2.50, $5, and $10 coins. By the mid-1800s, the Mint was producing about 17 million coins annually in 12 denominations.

Over the years, the Mint has made various adjustments and revisions to U.S. coinage in response to economic conditions prevailing at the time and the cost and supply of the metals from which the coins are produced. Gold and silver equally represented the base unit of value in the original U.S. monetary system, but the two precious metals had a troubled marriage through the years. At various times, the bimetallic system led to class warfare and private profiteering under the guise of public policy. From the beginning, some officials expressed concern about the system. They feared that world market fluctuations in the prices for the two metals would cause the more valuable metal to leave the country. Indeed, that's what happened in the early 1800s. The silver dollar coin intrinsically became less valuable than a dollar's worth of gold. Gold coins either disappeared quickly after minting or never entered circulation.

The situation was eased somewhat when gold was discovered in South Carolina in 1824 and Georgia in 1830. Then in 1834, a new law lowered the standard weight of all gold coins and established a gold-to-silver value ratio of 16.002-to-1. Five dollars in silver coins bought a new, lighter gold $5 coin. Speculators hoarded the older, heavier gold coins and hauled them to the melting pot at a profit of 4.7 percent. Follow-up legislation in 1837 established a uniform fineness of 0.900 for gold and silver coins, and tweaked the ratio again, to 15.998-to-1.

By the 1850s, the situation reversed. The discovery of gold in California made silver the more valuable metal, and silver coins became scarce in circulation. New gold $1 and $20 coins were authorized in 1849. Four years later, Congress lowered the weights of the half dime, dime, quarter, and half dollar to try to keep silver coins in circulation.

But by the mid-1870s, the situation reversed again when the Comstock Lode near Virginia City, Nev., dumped new, large supplies of silver on the market. Combined with European demonetization of silver, the bottom fell out of the metal's price.

The Coinage Act of 1873 brought sweeping changes to the U.S. monetary and coinage systems, and to the Mint's governing structure. First, the act established the main mint at Philadelphia and the various branch mints as a bureau of the Treasury Department to be headed by a director appointed by the president. Second, it authorized the minting of the following gold coins: $2.50,

$3, $5, $10, and $20. Third, it effectively put the nation on the gold standard, thus ending the bimetallic standard, and discontinued the silver dollar.

Those in favor of the legislation argued that the gold dollar was already the de facto standard for the U.S. monetary system and was consistent with the gold standard of Great Britain and most other European nations. Several years later, however, despite historical evidence to the contrary, silver interests insisted the gold standard and elimination of the silver dollar were secretly slipped into the legislation. Their cause was bolstered when a special congressional commission in 1877 concluded that the demonetization of silver had been effected solely to benefit the creditor classes.

The anti-gold-standard crowd advocated the resumption of large-scale silver-dollar production as a cheaper, more plentiful form of money in response to the era's economic woes. Their efforts resulted in the passage of what is commonly called today the Bland-Allison Act of 1878, which required the government to purchase $2 million to $4 million of silver monthly and resume the production of silver dollars for circulation.

In 1890, the Sherman Silver Purchase Act increased the required monthly purchases of silver to $4.5 million. By 1893, the intrinsic value of a silver dollar dropped to 52 cents. Holders of Treasury notes, redeemable in either silver or gold, chose the higher-valued gold for redemption and drained the Treasury's reserves of the yellow metal. President Grover Cleveland reported that from July 1, 1890, to July 15, 1893, the Treasury's gold reserves had decreased more than $132 million while its silver reserves increased more than $147 million. Later in 1893, Congress repealed the Sherman Silver Purchase Act.

In 1900, Congress confirmed the gold standard through legislation and directed the Treasury secretary to "maintain all forms of money in parity with this standard." The United States continued to issue gold coins into the 1900s, but the economic demands of World War I and then the economic challenges of the 1930s eventually led to the demise of the gold standard and the production of gold coins for circulation. In 1933, President Franklin D. Roosevelt banned the private ownership of gold bullion, and the production of U.S. gold coinage for circulation ceased. This and other actions effectively took the United States off the gold standard. In 1971, President Richard M. Nixon announced the United States would no longer exchange paper currency for gold in international transactions among central banks, which was the final step in the country abandoning the gold standard. In 1975, the United States lifted the restrictions on private ownership of gold bullion.

Another big change in U.S. coinage occurred in 1965. Until that year, dimes, quarters, and half dollars were still struck in the traditional composition of 90 percent silver and 10 percent copper. But by 1964, it cost the government more than 25 cents to produce a quarter because of rising silver prices. The high cost of silver coupled with increasing demand for coinage, in part from the growing popularity of vending machines, led to a coin shortage in the country.

In response, President Lyndon Johnson signed into law the Coinage Act of 1965, which eliminated silver from the dime and quarter, and replaced it with a clad composition consisting largely of copper, which continues to be used today. The half dollar was struck in a 40 percent silver composition from 1965 through 1970 before it, too, succumbed to the clad composition starting in 1971.

Even the lowly 1 cent coin has seen changes over the years in response to the supply and demand of metals. The early U.S. cents ranged in diameter from 26 to 29 millimeters and were composed of 100 percent copper. With the introduction of the Flying Eagle cent in 1856, the diameter was reduced to 19 millimeters and the composition to 88 percent copper.

Numerous composition changes in the cent ensued over the years. Although the 19-millimeter size continues, today's 1 cent coin is produced in copper-plated zinc.

The most recent trend in modern U.S. coinage is circulating issues with commemorative and collectible aspects. Prominent among them are the 50 State quarters, issued from 1999 to 2008. Also among them are the Westward Journey nickels (2004-2006) and the Lincoln Bicentennial cents (2009). The America the Beautiful quarters series, which commemorates the nation's national parks and sites, began in 2010 and is scheduled to run through 2021.

HOW TO COLLECT COINS

A coin collection can be whatever an individual wants it to be. Collect what you like and what brings you pleasure as a leisure-time hobby. It's also good to have a strategy and a road map to your collecting pursuits. Thus, following are some tips and comments on traditional collecting strategies.

By series. The traditional coin-collecting pursuit of acquiring one example of each date and mintmark within a particular series may seem daunting at first considering the long runs of some U.S. coin series. To get started, a collector can break down a series into smaller parts. For example, a collector interested in Lincoln cents can start with those depicting the Lincoln Memorial on the reverse, which began in 1959. A collector can also get started by collecting simply one date of each Lincoln Memorial cent rather than seeking an example of every mintmark of a particular date.

U.S. MINTMARKS

C	Charlotte, N.C. (1838-1861)
CC	Carson City, Nev. (1870-1893)
D	Dahlonega, Ga. (1838-1861)
D	Denver (1906-present)
O	New Orleans (1838-1909)
P	Philadelphia (1793-present)
S	San Francisco (1854-present)
W	West Point, N.Y. (1984-present)

Coins without mintmarks were struck at Philadelphia.

By type. Rather than seeking an example of every date and mintmark within a series, many collectors seek just one example of each type of coin within a particular focus. For example, a collector assembling a 20th century type set of U.S. 5-cent coins would seek one Liberty nickel, one Buffalo nickel, and one Jefferson nickel. The representative coins could be of any date and mintmark within each series, thus accommodating any collecting budget.

By theme. The proliferation of modern commemorative and circulating commemorative coins gave rise to collecting coins with a common theme. Examples include coins that depict animals or ships, coins that commemorate a certain event, or coins of a certain date, such as 2000.

By collector's choice. Various aspects of the listed strategies overlap and can be combined and mixed to form a goal that interests an individual collector. The result should be a coin collection that is affordable and attainable for the collector, and a collection that brings enjoyment and satisfaction.

HOW TO HANDLE COINS

The less coins are handled, the better. Dirty, oily hands – even if they appear to be clean – lead to dirty, oily coins. Oftentimes, however, coins have to be handled, particularly when searching circulating coins or when transferring a coin to a holder. When it is necessary to handle a coin, it should be held by the edges between the thumb and forefinger. Avoid contact with the coin's obverse and reverse surfaces.

Also, handle coins over a soft surface so they will not be damaged if accidentally dropped.

Should I clean my coins?

No.

Luster is an important aspect when grading certain high-end coins, but in general, a coin's grade and its corresponding value depend on the amount of wear on the coin, not how shiny it is. Cleaning – particularly home-brewed methods – is often abrasive and will damage a coin rather than improve it.

There may be certain instances when it is desirable to clean a coin, but that is best left to experienced opinions as to when and how.

HOW TO STORE COINS

Folders. Cardboard folders are the most inexpensive and common form of organizing and storing a collection. They can be purchased at many hobby shops and bookstores.

They provide a spot for each date and mintmark in a particular series, thus acting as a road map for the collector. They are also compact and convenient; they take up little space on a bookshelf and can be pulled down and opened for easy viewing.

The spots for the coins consist of holes in the cardboard sized specially for the particular series covered by the folder. They are meant to be a tight fit so the coins, once inserted, won't fall out. Place the coin in the hole at an angle, so one side of the coin is in the hole. On the side of the coin sticking up, press down and toward the angled side until the coin snaps into place.

The process isn't always graceful; thus, some of the basic rules for handling coins have to be suspended when working with folders. But folders are still suitable for storing coins plucked from circulation and getting started in coin collecting.

2-by-2s. Low to moderately priced coins offered for sale at shops and shows are usually stored in cardboard holders commonly called "2-by-2s" because they are 2 inches square. They consist of two pieces with a clear Mylar window in the center. The coin is placed between the two pieces, which are then stapled together.

These 2-by-2 holders are also inexpensive. They are suitable for long-term storage and offer a number of advantages over the basic folder:

• The window in the holder allows both sides of the coin to be viewed.

• The entire coin is enclosed.

• The coin can be handled by the edges when being inserted into the holder.

As for disadvantages:

• Storing an entire collection of a particular series takes up more space.

• The coins can be viewed only one at a time.

• Caution should be used when inserting or removing coins from the holders to make sure the staples' sharp edges don't damage the coins.

• There is no road map to the series. A separate checklist is needed.

The 2-by-2 holders can be stored in long, narrow boxes specially sized to hold them. They can also be inserted into pockets in a plastic page, which can then be inserted into a three-ring binder.

Originally the plastic pages contained polyvinylchloride, which produced a soft, flexible pocket. But the substance breaks down over time, resulting in a green slime that could contact the coins. Manufacturers then started substituting Mylar for the PVC. The Mylar does not break down, but the page containing it is more brittle and not as flexible.

Flips. Similar in size to the cardboard 2-by-2s, plastic "flips," to use the vernacular, are another common storage method for coins for sale. They consist of a plastic pocket, into which the coin is inserted, with a flap that folds down over the pocket. Coin dealers will often staple the flap shut.

Flips offer many of the same advantages as the cardboard 2-by-2s:

- Although they cost more, flips are still inexpensive.
- The entire coin is enclosed.
- Both sides of the coin can be viewed.
- The coin can be handled by the edges when being inserted into the holder.

Also, they don't have to be stapled shut, thus eliminating the possibility of the staples scratching the coin.

The big disadvantage to flips is their composition. They, too, originally contained polyvinylchloride. Manufacturers then started making flips containing Mylar, but the resulting product again is more brittle and not as flexible as the old PVC flips.

For long-term storage, it's best to remove coins from flips and transfer them to another type of holder.

Albums. Coin albums are a step up from the basic folder. They are in book form and contain a hole for each date and mintmark in the particular series covered. The hole has a clear plastic back and a clear plastic front. The plastic front slides out, and the coin can be placed in the hole. The plastic front is then slid back over the hole.

Albums combine many of the advantages of 2-by-2s and folders:

- They are compact and convenient, and can be stored on a bookshelf.
- They are affordable.
- Both sides of the coin can be viewed.

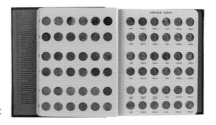

- Their labeled holes act as a road map to a series.
- The entire coin is enclosed.
- The coin can be handled by the edges when being inserted.

The disadvantage to albums is that sliding the plastic front can damage a coin in the holder if the plastic rubs against the coin. Thus, albums are not recommended for expensive uncirculated coins.

Hard-plastic holders. Hard-plastic holders are the top of the line in coin stortage, but are still affordable. They consist of two pieces with one or more clear windows through which the coin can be viewed. The two pieces are held together with plastic screws or snap together.

To insert a coin into the holder, the two pieces are separated, and the coin is placed face up into the bottom piece. The top piece is then placed over the bottom piece, and the two pieces are screwed or snapped together again.

Some of the world's great numismatic rarities are stored in hard-plastic holders. They offer all of the advantages of the less expensive storage methods but in a safe, inert environment.

Slabs. In 1986, a group of coin dealers got together and formed the Professional Coin Grading Service. For a fee, dealers and collectors could submit coins to the service and receive a professional opinion on their grades. After grading, a coin is encapsulated in an inert hard-plastic holder with a serial number and the service's opinion on its grade indicated on the holder.

The concept was successful, and several competing services were established in succeeding years. Today, most coins valuable enough to justify the grading fee have been graded by one of the services and encapsulated in its holder.

The grading-service holders are common at coin shows and shops, and acquired the nickname "slabs." The holders are suitable for long-term storage of high-end collectible coins.

ABOUT THE VALUE LISTINGS

Coin values listed in this book are estimated retail prices. These are the approximate prices collectors can expect to pay when buying the listed coins in the listed grades from dealers at shows and shops, and through advertisements in coin-collecting magazines.

The date in individual listings is the date on the coin or the year in which the coin was issued in those instances where coins are not dated. A letter following the date indicates the mintmark on the coin.

Many design varieties of early U.S. coinage may exist for particular dates of coins. Rarer varieties and those with no significant difference in value are not listed.

Grading U.S. coins

A coin's value is determined in part by its grade, or state of preservation. Grading terms provide a concise method for describing a coin's condition, particularly when a dealer or collector advertises a coin for sale in a magazine. Several grading-guide books, which illustrate and describe U.S. coins in different series in different grades, are commonly used by dealers and collectors. Among them is *The Official American Numismatic Association Grading Standards for United States Coins.*

Following are commonly used grading terms and a general description of each:

Uncirculated (unc.), or mint state (MS), coins have no wear on them. Mint state coins are further graded on a numerical scale from 60 to 70, with MS-70 being theoretical perfection. Although mint state coins may show no wear from circulation, they can still vary in condition. For example, after coins are struck, they are loaded into bags and then shipped from the mint. Scuff marks occur when the coins bang into each other while being shipped in the bags. Although the coins may not show wear from circulation, these "bag marks" can detract from their condition.

Some professional grading services use all 11 increments from 60 to 70 in grading mint state coins. Some traditionalists, however, believe it's impossible to tell a one-point difference in mint state grades. The ANA grading guide, for example, lists and describes only MS-60, MS-63, MS-65, and MS-67.

Brilliant uncirculated (BU) refers to a mint state coin retaining all or most of its original luster. It may have a numeric grade of MS-60 to MS-70. For higher grades, many dealers prefer to use the more precise numeric grades.

MS-67 is the closest thing to perfection that is likely to appear on the market. An MS-67 coin may have the faintest of bag marks, which can be seen only with a magnifying glass. An MS-67 copper coin must retain its original luster.

MS-65 describes an exceptional coin and often is the highest grade used when grading conservatively. It will have no significant bag marks, particularly in open areas such as the field or the cheek of a person portrayed on the coin. An MS-65 copper coin may be toned.

MS-63 coins are pleasant, collectible examples that exhibit enough bag marks to be noticed but not so many that coins are considered marred. Bag marks should be especially few in open areas, such as the fields or a cheek.

MS-60 describes a coin that saw considerable scuffing at the mint before its release. It will often have nicks and discoloration. Some high-grade circulated coins may be more attractive than some MS-60 coins.

About uncirculated (AU or AU-50) coins have slight signs of wear. A magnifying glass may be needed to see them. A trace of original luster should be visible. Care should be taken not to mistake an AU coin for an uncirculated coin.

Extremely fine (EF or XF, or EF-40 or XF-40) describes a coin that retains clear detail in its design but shows wear that can be seen without a magnifying glass. For U.S. coins with the word "Liberty" on a headband or shield, all letters must be sharp and clear. Some XF coins may still have original luster, but it is not necessary for the coin to meet this grade.

Very fine (VF or VF-20) coins show obvious signs of wear, but most design details are still clear, making for an overall pleasant coin. All letters must be clear in the word "Liberty" on a headband or shield.

Fine (F or F-12) is the lowest grade most people consider collectible. An F coin retains about half of its design details. All letters in the word "Liberty" on a headband or shield must be visible but may not be sharp.

Very good (VG or VG-8) coins exhibit heavy wear. All outlines in the design are clear along with the rim. Some design details are also retained but most are worn. At least three letters in the word "Liberty" on a headband or shield must be legible. On a pre-1857 copper coin or Morgan dollar, all of the letters in "Liberty" must be present.

Good (G or G-4) describes a coin with no internal detail remaining. Some of the rim may also be worn down. The word "Liberty," if originally present, will be worn off or just trace elements remaining on pre-1857 copper coins and Morgan dollars.

Proof (PF) describes a process of manufacture rather than a grade. Proof coins are struck from specially selected, highly polished planchets and dies. They usually receive multiple strikes from the coining press at increased pressure. The result is a coin with mirrorlike surfaces and, in recent years, a cameo effect on its raised design surfaces.

Under the ANA grading system, proof grades use the same numbers as circulated and uncirculated grades, and the amount of wear on the coin corresponds to those grades. But the number is preceded by the word "proof" – proof-65, proof-55, proof-45, and so on. The ANA says a proof coin with many marks, scratches, or other defects should be called an "impaired proof."

To command the values listed in this book, proof coins should meet the proof-65 or higher standard.

Half cents

Half cents are much more popular among collectors today than they were in circulation when issued. The small-denomination coins permitted precise dealings in commerce, but they were considered nuisances by those who had to handle them. Demand for half cents in circulation was low, which kept mintages low. In some years, none was struck. In other years, the U.S. Mint didn't allocate any blanks for them and struck them on second-hand merchant tokens instead.

Though not as popularly collected as large cents, half cents today are considered scarce and desirable. Like large cents, half cents are collected by die variety. Rare die combinations can be worth much more than common ones of the same year. Early dates are scarce in better grades. The Classic Head type is much easier to find in better grades.

LIBERTY CAP

Head facing left

Size: *22 millimeters.* **Weight:** *6.74 grams.* **Composition:** *100 percent copper.*

	VG	VF
1793	5,350	15,000

LIBERTY CAP

Head facing right

	VG	VF
1794	650	1,600
1795	475	1,500
1796 with pole	20,000	30,000

	VG	VF
1796 no pole	35,500	90,000
1797	475	1,600

DRAPED BUST

Size: *23.5 millimeters.* **Weight:** *5.44 grams.* **Composition:** *100 percent copper.*

	VG	VF
1800	90.00	200
1802	1,400	6,500
1803	95.00	575
1804	90.00	200
1805	90.00	200
1805 small 5, stems at wreath	1,500	4,500

	VG	VF
1806	85.00	215
1806 small 6, stems at wreath	355	1,000
1807	95.00	220
1808	85.00	215

CLASSIC HEAD

Size: *23.5 millimeters.* **Weight:** *5.44 grams.* **Composition:** *100 percent copper.*

	VG	VF
1809	80.00	110
1810	100	500
1811	375	1,800
1825	75.00	110
1826	70.00	90.00
1828 13 stars	70.00	85.00
1828 12 stars	80.00	175
1829	70.00	100
1831 original	—	*XF* 65,000

	VG	VF
1831 restrike	—	*unc.* 6,500
1832	70.00	85.00
1833	70.00	85.00
1834	70.00	85.00
1835	70.00	85.00
1836 original	—	*proof* 6,000
1836 restrike	—	*proof* 50,000

BRAIDED HAIR

Size: *23 millimeters.* **Weight:** *5.44 grams.* **Composition:** *100 percent copper.*
Notes: *The 1840-1849 issues, 1849 small-date variety, and 1852, both originals and restrikes, are known in proof only. The restrikes were produced clandestinely by Philadelphia Mint personnel in the mid-1800s.*

	VG	VF	PF-60
1840 original	3,250		
1840 1st restrike	3,250		
1840 2nd restrike			5,500
1841 original	3,250		
1841 1st restrike	3,250		
1841 2nd restrike	6,000		
1842 original	3,250		
1842 1st restrike	3,250		
1842 2nd restrike	6,000		
1843 original	3,250		
1843 1st restrike	3,250		
1843 2nd restrike	6,500		
1844 original	3,250		
1844 1st restrike	3,250		
1844 2nd restrike	6,000		
1845 original	6,000		
1845 1st restrike	3,250		
1845 2nd restrike	6,000		

	VG	VF	PF-60
1846 original	3,250		
1846 1st restrike	3,250		
1846 2nd restrike	6,000		
1847 original	3,250		
1847 1st restrike	3,250		
1847 2nd restrike	6,000		
1848 original	6,000		
1848 1st restrike	3,250		
1848 2nd restrike	6,000		
1849 original, small date	3,250		
1849 1st restrike, small date			3,250
1849 large date	90.00		75.00
1850	90.00		75.00
1851	85.00		70.00
1852 original		35,000	25,000
1852 1st restrike	1,500	2,600	
1852 2nd restrike	2,600		1,500
1853	85.00		70.00
1854	85.00		70.00
1855	85.00		70.00
1856	85.00		70.00
1857	100		75.00

Large cents

The large cent resulted from the desire for a decimal coin worth 100th of a dollar and the need for a coin to replace British halfpennies and their imitations, which were common in the Colonies. The large cent was slightly larger than the halfpenny.

Early American coin dies were engraved by hand, so no two were identical. Because of this, collecting large cents by die variety is popular. Rare die combinations are worth more than the common ones of the same year.

Low mintages and lukewarm acceptance by the public caused the first large cents to be little more than local Philadelphia coinage. Metal was in such short supply that junked copper hardware of inconsistent alloy was used for some early cents. As a result, some early large cents were struck on blanks of poor quality.

The chain design on the reverse of the first large cents was criticized as anti-liberty. The frightened expression on Liberty's face was also panned.

Later, it was popular to nail large cents to the rafters of new houses for good luck. These "rafter cents" are devalued today because of the square nail holes in them, but they still have some value as historical novelties.

The large cent was discontinued after 1857 for the more convenient small cent.

Early large cents are difficult to find in better grades.

FLOWING HAIR

Chain

Size: *26-27 millimeters.* **Weight:** *13.48 grams.* **Composition:** *100 percent copper.*

	VG	VF
1793 "AMERI"	13,750	45,500
1793 "AMERICA"	10,500	36,500
1793 periods after "LIBERTY"	11,250	38,500

Wreath

Size: *26-28 millimeters.* **Weight:** *13.48 grams.* **Composition:** *100 percent copper.*

	VG	VF
1793 vine-and-bars edge	2,950	7,500
1793 lettered edge	3,250	8,000

LIBERTY CAP

Size: *29 millimeters.* **Weight:** *13.48 grams (1793-1795) and 10.89 grams (1795-1796).*
Composition: *100 percent copper.* **Notes:** *The Liberty design on the obverse
was revised slightly in 1794, but the 1793 design was used on some 1794 strikes.
The 1795 lettered-edge variety has "ONE HUNDRED FOR A DOLLAR"
and a leaf inscribed on the edge.*

	VG	VF
1793	6,500	36,500
1794	550	1,550
1794 head of 1793	2,600	8,450

	VG	VF
1795	455	1,450
1795 lettered edge	480	1,850
1796	450	4,000

DRAPED BUST

Size: *29 millimeters.* **Weight:** *10.98 grams.* **Composition:** *100 percent copper.*

	VG	VF
1796	350	1,500
1797	225	1,000
1798	130	350
1799	4,650	24,500
1800	130	650
1801	85.00	375
1802	85.00	360

	VG	VF
1803 small date	85.00	350
1803 large date	6,950	26,500
1804	2,650	8,950
1805	90.00	300
1806	100	375
1807	85.00	350

CLASSIC HEAD

Size: *29 millimeters.* **Weight:** *10.89 grams.* **Composition:** *100 percent copper.*

	VG	VF
1808	150	575
1809	250	1,050
1810	95.00	550
1811	175	1,000

	VG	VF
1812	90.00	550
1813	175	800
1814	90.00	550

Size: *28-29 millimeters.* **Weight:** *10.89 grams.* **Composition:** *100 percent copper.*

	VG	VF
1816	35.00	115
1817 13 obverse stars	35.00	70.00
1817 15 obverse stars	45.00	165
1818	35.00	70.00
1819	35.00	70.00
1820	35.00	70.00
1821	75.00	400
1822	35.00	100
1823	200	700
1824	35.00	160
1825	35.00	110
1826	35.00	85.00

	VG	VF
1827	35.00	90.00
1828	35.00	90.00
1829	35.00	90.00
1830	30.00	70.00
1831	30.00	70.00
1832	30.00	70.00
1833	30.00	70.00
1834	30.00	70.00
1835	30.00	70.00
1836	30.00	70.00
1837	30.00	70.00
1838	30.00	70.00
1839	35.00	75.00

BRAIDED HAIR

Size: *27.5 millimeters.* **Weight:** *10.89 grams.* **Composition:** *100 percent copper.*

	VG	VF
1839	35.00	40.00
1840	30.00	35.00
1841	30.00	40.00
1842	30.00	35.00
1843	30.00	35.00
1844	30.00	35.00
1845	30.00	35.00
1846	25.00	35.00
1847	25.00	35.00
1848	30.00	35.00
1849	30.00	35.00
1850	30.00	35.00
1851	25.00	35.00

	VG	VF
1852	25.00	35.00
1853	25.00	35.00
1854	25.00	35.00
1855 slanted 5s	55.00	70.00
1855 upright 5s	25.00	35.00
1856 slanted 5	25.00	35.00
1856 upright 5	40.00	55.00
1857 large date	150	235
1857 small date	110	190

Small cents

FLYING EAGLE

Americans gladly accepted the new, smaller Flying Eagle cents when they were introduced to replace the bulkier large cents. An estimated 2,500 1856-dated Flying Eagle cents were produced before the law authorizing the coin was actually passed. Technically, that makes them patterns, but they are widely listed with the regular production issues of 1857 and 1858, and are commonly considered part of this short-lived series. Collectors should watch for genuine 1857 and 1858 Flying Eagle cents with their dates re-engraved to read 1856.

Size: *19 millimeters.* **Weight:** *4.67 grams.*
Composition: *88 percent copper, 12 percent nickel.*

	VG	VF
1856	7,250	10,750
1857	40.00	45.00
1858	45.00	50.00

INDIAN HEAD

The Indian Head cent was popularly named for the image of Liberty wearing an American Indian headdress on the obverse. Legend has it that the coin's designer, James B. Longacre, was inspired to create the image when an Indian chief visiting the U.S. Mint took off his headdress and placed it on the head of Longacre's daughter Sarah. It's a charming tale but probably not true. The Indian Head cent's reverse was changed after just one year of production. In 1860, an oak wreath replaced the laurel wreath in the original design and a shield was added at the top. A composition change also occurred in 1864.

Size: *19 millimeters.* **Weight:** *4.67 grams.* **Composition:** *88 percent copper, 12 percent nickel (1859-1864) and 95 percent copper, 5 percent tin and zinc (bronze, 1864-1909).* **Notes:** *A shield was added at the top of the reverse in 1860.*

	F	XF			F	XF
1859	25.00	100		1867	110	195
1860	20.00	70.00		1868	75.00	180
1861	40.00	95.00		1869	230	450
1862	12.50	30.00		1870	225	410
1863	11.00	25.00		1871	280	420
1864 copper-nickel	35.00	125		1872	390	625
1864 bronze	25.00	70.00		1873	65.00	175
1865	20.00	45.00		1874	45.00	110
1866	80.00	195		1875	55.00	120

	F	XF
1876	75.00	230
1877	1,600	2,650
1878	70.00	245
1879	16.50	75.00
1880	6.50	30.00
1881	6.50	20.00
1882	5.00	20.00
1883	4.50	17.50
1884	7.00	30.00
1885	12.00	60.00
1886	20.00	150
1887	4.00	20.00
1888	5.00	20.00
1889	3.50	12.00
1890	3.00	10.00
1891	3.25	13.00
1892	4.50	18.50
1893	3.25	10.00

	F	XF
1894	13.00	50.00
1895	3.50	11.00
1896	3.25	13.00
1897	2.75	10.00
1898	2.75	10.00
1899	2.50	10.00
1900	2.50	12.00
1901	2.50	11.00
1902	2.50	10.00
1903	2.50	10.00
1904	2.50	10.00
1905	2.50	9.00
1906	2.50	9.00
1907	2.50	8.50
1908	2.50	9.00
1908-S	100	165
1909-S	720	900
1909	15.50	18.50

LINCOLN

The Lincoln cent was introduced in 1909 to mark the centennial of Abraham Lincoln's birth. Lincoln thus became the first president, and the first real person, to be depicted on a circulating U.S. coin. The coin's original reverse design consisted of two wheat ears framing the words "One Cent." It was changed to a depiction of the Lincoln Memorial in 1959 to mark the 150th anniversary of Lincoln's birth. In 2009, the U.S. Mint struck the Lincoln cent with four different reverses to mark the bicentennial of Lincoln's birth.

The Lincoln cent has also seen several composition changes over the years. In 1943, Lincoln cents were produced in zinc-coated steel to conserve copper for the war effort. Later composition changes were in response to rising prices for copper.

Wheat reverse

Size: *19 millimeters.* **Weight:** *3.11 grams.* **Composition:** *95 percent copper, 5 percent tin and zinc.* **Notes:** *The 1909 "VDB" varieties have the designer's initials inscribed at the 6 o'clock position on the reverse. The initials were removed until 1918, when they were placed on the obverse.*

	VF	MS-60
1909 VDB	13.50	25.00
1909-S VDB	1,175	1,825
1909	4.75	14.50
1909-S	165	350
1910	1.00	17.50
1910-S	28.00	100
1911	2.50	18.50
1911-D	25.00	90.00
1911-S	60.00	175
1912	5.50	35.00

	VF	MS-60
1912-D	25.00	160
1912-S	45.00	175
1913	3.25	35.00
1913-D	10.50	100.00
1913-S	30.00	195
1914	6.00	50.00
1914-D	450	2,100
1914-S	40.00	310
1915	18.00	80.00
1915-D	7.00	70.00

	VF	MS-60		VF	MS-60
1915-S	30.00	190	1926-S	16.50	140
1916	2.50	20.00	1927	0.60	7.50
1916-D	6.50	90.00	1927-D	3.50	60.00
1916-S	9.50	100	1927-S	5.25	65.00
1917	2.00	18.50	1928	0.60	7.50
1917-D	5.00	70.00	1928-D	3.75	35.00
1917-S	2.50	75.00	1929	0.50	7.00
1918	1.00	13.50	1929-D	2.75	25.00
1918-D	5.50	75.00	1929-S	2.75	20.00
1918-S	3.75	65.00	1930	0.60	4.00
1919	1.00	8.00	1930-D	0.90	11.00
1919-D	5.00	60.00	1930-S	0.80	9.50
1919-S	2.50	50.00	1931	2.00	20.00
1920	1.25	15.00	1931-D	8.00	50.00
1920-D	7.00	70.00	1931-S	125	160
1920-S	2.75	100	1932	3.50	17.50
1921	3.00	40.00	1932-D	2.85	18.50
1921-S	6.25	110	1933	2.85	16.50
1922-D	25.00	100	1933-D	7.50	25.00
1923	1.50	13.50	1934	0.50	9.00
1923-S	12.50	190	1934-D	1.25	20.00
1924	1.00	17.50	1935	0.50	5.00
1924-D	60.00	255	1935-D	0.50	5.50
1924-S	5.50	110	1935-S	1.75	11.00
1925	0.75	9.50	1936-D	0.50	4.00
1925-D	6.25	60.00	1936-S	0.60	5.00
1925-S	2.75	85.00	1937	0.50	1.75
1926	0.60	7.50	1937-D	0.60	2.75
1926-D	5.25	80.00	1937-S	0.50	2.75

	VF	MS-60
1938	0.50	2.25
1938-D	0.60	3.50
1938-S	0.70	3.00
1939	0.50	1.00
1939-D	0.60	3.00
1939-S	0.60	2.50
1940	0.40	1.00
1940-D	0.50	2.00

	VF	MS-60
1940-S	0.50	2.50
1941	0.40	1.25
1941-D	0.50	2.25
1941-S	0.50	2.50
1942	0.40	0.85
1942-D	0.35	1.00
1942-S	0.85	5.00

Steel composition

Size: *19 millimeters.* **Weight:** *2.7 grams.* **Composition:** *Zinc-coated steel.*

	VF	MS-60
1943	0.45	1.25
1943-D	0.50	1.50
1943-S	0.65	4.00

Copper-zinc composition

Size: *19 millimeters.* **Weight:** *3.11 grams.* **Composition:** *95 percent copper, 5 percent zinc.*

	XF-40	MS-65
1944	0.40	8.00
1944-D	0.50	12.50
1944-S	0.40	11.00
1945	0.40	13.50
1945-D	0.40	12.50

	XF-40	MS-65
1945-S	0.40	8.50
1946	0.30	9.00
1946-D	0.30	10.00
1946-S	0.30	12.00
1947	0.45	10.00

	XF-40	MS-65
1947-D	0.40	9.00
1947-S	0.35	12.00
1948	0.40	10.00
1948-D	0.40	7.00
1948-S	0.40	8.00
1949	0.40	12.50
1949-D	0.40	15.00
1949-S	0.50	10.00
1950	0.40	13.50
1950-D	0.35	7.50
1950-S	0.40	9.00
1951	0.40	14.00
1951-D	0.30	8.50
1951-S	0.40	10.00
1952	0.40	16.00
1952-D	0.30	8.50

	XF-40	MS-65
1952-S	0.60	12.00
1953	0.30	15.00
1953-D	0.30	9.50
1953-S	0.40	10.00
1954	0.25	14.00
1954-D	0.25	10.00
1954-S	0.25	12.00
1955	0.25	15.00
1955-D	0.20	12.00
1955-S	0.35	12.00
1956	0.20	16.00
1956-D	0.20	8.00
1957	0.20	9.00
1957-D	0.20	8.00
1958	0.20	9.00
1958-D	0.20	8.00

Lincoln Memorial reverse

Size: *19 millimeters.* **Weight:** *3.11 grams.* **Composition:** *95 percent copper, 5 percent zinc.*

	MS-65	PF-65
1959	18.00	10.00
1959-D	16.00	—
1960 small date	12.00	18.00
1960 large date	10.00	10.00

	MS-65	PF-65
1960-D small date	10.00	—
1960-D large date	11.00	—
1961	6.50	9.00

	MS-65	PF-65
1961-D	15.00	—
1962	8.00	8.00
1962-D	14.00	—
1963	10.00	8.00
1963-D	12.00	—
1964	6.50	8.00
1964-D	7.00	—
1965	10.00	—
1966	10.00	—
1967	10.00	—
1968	12.00	—
1968-D	12.00	—
1968-S	8.00	1.00
1969	6.50	—
1969-D	10.00	—
1969-S	8.00	1.10
1970	8.00	—
1970-D	6.00	—
1970-S	—	1.25
1970-S small date	75.00	60.00
1970-S large date	16.00	—
1971	25.00	—
1971-D	5.50	—
1971-S	6.00	1.25
1972	6.00	—
1972-D	10.00	—
1972-S	30.00	1.15
1973	8.00	—

	MS-65	PF-65
1973-D	11.00	—
1973-D	8.00	0.80
1974	12.00	—
1974-D	12.00	—
1974-S	10.00	0.75
1975	8.00	—
1975-D	13.50	—
1975-S	—	5.50
1976	18.00	—
1976-D	20.00	—
1976-S	—	5.00
1977	0.25	—
1977-D	0.25	—
1977-S	—	3.00
1978	0.25	—
1978-D	0.25	—
1978-S	—	3.50
1979	0.25	—
1979-D	0.25	—
1979-S	—	4.25
1980	0.25	—
1980-D	0.25	—
1980-S	—	2.25
1981	0.25	—
1981-D	0.25	—
1981-S	—	3.50
1982	0.25	—
1982-D	0.25	—
1982-S	—	3.00

Copper-plated zinc composition

Size: *19 millimeters.* **Weight:** *2.5 grams.* **Composition:** *97.6 percent zinc, 2.4 percent copper.*

	MS-65	PF-65			MS-65	PF-65
1982 large date	0.30	—		1989	0.25	—
1982 small date	2.00	—		1989-D	0.25	—
1982-D large date	8.00	—		1989-S	—	6.00
1982-D small date	0.30	—		1990	0.25	—
1982-S	—	3.00		1990-D	0.25	—
1983	0.25	—		1990-S	—	5.00
1983-D	0.50	—		1991	0.25	—
1983-S	—	4.00		1991-D	0.25	—
1984	0.25	—		1991-S	—	5.00
1984-D	0.75	—		1992	0.25	—
1984-S	—	4.50		1992-D	0.25	—
1985	0.25	—		1992-S	—	5.00
1985-D	0.25	—		1993	0.25	—
1985-S	—	6.00		1993-D	0.25	—
1986	1.50	—		1993-S	—	7.00
1986-D	1.25	—		1994	0.25	—
1986-S	—	7.50		1994-D	0.25	—
1987	0.25	—		1994-S	—	4.00
1987-D	0.25	—		1995	0.25	—
1987-S	—	5.00		1995-D	0.25	—
1988	0.25	—		1995-S	—	9.50
1988-D	0.25	—		1996	0.25	—
1988-S	—	4.00		1996-D	0.25	—
				1996-S	—	6.50
				1997	0.25	—

	MS-65	PF-65
1997-D	0.25	—
1997-S	—	11.50
1998	0.25	—
1998-D	0.25	—
1998-S	—	9.50
1999	0.25	—
1999-D	0.25	—
1999-S	—	5.00
2000	0.25	—
2000-D	0.25	—
2000-S	—	4.00
2001	0.25	—
2001-D	0.25	—
2001-S	—	4.00
2002	0.25	—
2002-D	0.25	—
2002-S	—	4.00
2003	0.25	—

	MS-65	PF-65
2003-D	0.25	—
2003-S	—	4.00
2004	3.50	—
2004-D	0.25	—
2004-S	—	4.00
2005	0.25	—
2005-D	0.25	—
2005-S	—	4.00
2006	0.25	—
2006-D	0.25	—
2006-S	—	4.00
2007	1.50	—
2007-D	1.50	—
2007-S	—	4.00
2008	1.50	—
2008-D	1.50	—
2008-S	—	4.00

LINCOLN BICENTENNIAL

Lincoln Bicentennial cents designated as "copper" in the listings below were struck in the predominately copper composition used for the original Lincoln cents of 1909-1942. They were struck in proof and uncirculated versions for sale to collectors. The traditional bust of Lincoln was used on the obverse of all Lincoln bicentennial cents.

Log cabin

	MS-65	PF-65
2009-P	1.50	—
2009-P copper	1.50	—
2009-D	1.50	—

	MS-65	PF-65
2009-D copper	1.50	—
2009-S copper	—	4.00

Lincoln reading

	MS-65	PF-65
2009-P	1.50	—
2009-P copper	1.50	—
2009-D	1.50	—

	MS-65	PF-65
2009-D copper	1.50	—
2009-S copper	—	4.00

Illinois Old State Capitol

	MS-65	PF-65
2009-P	1.50	—
2009-P copper	1.50	—
2009-D	1.50	—
2009-D copper	1.50	—
2009-S copper	—	4.00

U.S. Capitol

	MS-65	PF-65
2009-P	1.50	—
2009-P copper	1.50	—
2009-D	1.50	—
2009-D copper	1.50	—
2009-S copper	—	4.00

UNION SHIELD REVERSE

Beginning in 2010, the Lincoln-cent reverse design symbolized Lincoln's preservation of the United States as a single, unified country. The design chosen shows a union shield with a scroll draped across it bearing the inscription "One Cent."

	MS-65	PF-65
2010-P	1.50	—
2010-D	1.50	—
2010-S	—	4.00
2011-P	1.50	—
2011-D	1.50	—
2011-S	—	4.00

TWO CENTS

The 2-cent piece is famous for being the first U.S. coin to carry the motto "In God We Trust." It was introduced in response to a shortage of small change during the Civil War.

Size: *23 millimeters.* **Weight:** *6.22 grams.* **Composition:** *95 percent copper, 5 percent tin and zinc.* **Notes:** *The motto "In God We Trust" was modified in 1864, resulting in small-motto and large-motto varieties for that year.*

	F	XF
1864 small motto	285	650
1864 large motto	20.00	45.00
1865	20.00	45.00
1866	20.00	45.00
1867	35.00	60.00
1868	35.00	65.00

	F	XF
1869	40.00	80.00
1870	60.00	135
1871	70.00	150
1872	700	1,200
1873 closed 3		*proof* 1,750
1873 open 3		*proof* 1,875

SILVER THREE CENTS

Silver 3-cent coins were issued to facilitate purchases of 3-cent postage stamps. In terms of size, they are the smallest coins in U.S. history and are also thin. They didn't strike up well, so today it's difficult to find fully struck examples with no weak spots in the design even in higher grades.

Type 1

Size: *14 millimeters.* **Weight:** *0.8 grams.* **Composition:** *75 percent silver (0.0193 troy ounces), 25 percent copper.* **Notes:** *The type 1 design has no outlines in the star.*

	F	XF
1851	50.00	70.00
1851-O	60.00	160

	F	XF
1852	50.00	70.00
1853	50.00	70.00

Type 2

Size: *14 millimeters.* **Weight:** *0.75 grams.* **Composition:** *90 percent silver (0.0218 troy ounces), 10 percent copper.* **Notes:** *The Type 2 design has three lines outlining the star.*

	F	XF
1854	50.00	150
1855	75.00	200
1856	55.00	120

	F	XF
1857	55.00	115
1858	50.00	120

Type 3

Size: 14 millimeters. **Weight:** 0.75 grams. **Composition:** 90 percent silver (0.0218 troy ounces), 10 percent copper. **Notes:** The Type 3 design has two lines outlining the star.

	F	XF
1859	50.00	85.00
1860	50.00	85.00
1861	50.00	85.00
1862	55.00	90.00
1863	450	520
1864	450	520
1865	550	665

	F	XF
1866	450	520
1867	575	675
1868	585	690
1869	585	690
1870	525	665
1871	535	670
1872	550	690

NICKEL THREE CENTS

Though produced concurrently for several years, the larger nickel 3-cent was intended to replace the smaller, more fragile silver 3-cent. Also, the nickel alloy saved the new coins from Civil War-era silver hoarders.

Size: *17.9 millimeters.* **Weight:** *1.94 grams.* **Composition:** *75 percent copper, 25 percent nickel.*

	F	XF		F	XF
1865	17.50	35.00	1878		proof 800
1866	17.50	35.00	1879	95.00	115
1867	17.50	35.00	1880	130	185
1868	17.50	35.00	1881	20.00	40.00
1869	19.50	40.00	1882	180	300
1870	20.00	40.00	1883	260	375
1871	25.00	45.00	1884	550	645
1872	25.00	45.00	1885	645	745
1873	20.00	40.00	1886		proof 385
1874	20.00	40.00	1887	400	455
1875	30.00	45.00	1888	70.00	100
1876	25.00	50.00	1889	140	220
1877		proof 1,300			

Half dimes

The half dime was one of the denominations originally authorized in 1792. The first examples were not struck until February 1795, but were dated 1794. Their designs emulated those on the larger dime. Half dimes were thin and susceptible to bending and dents in circulation.

FLOWING HAIR

Size: *16.5 millimeters.* **Weight:** *1.35 grams.* **Composition:** *89.24 percent silver (0.0388 troy ounces), 10.76 percent copper.*

	VG	VF
1794	1,625	3,125
1795	1,350	2,850

DRAPED BUST

Small eagle

Size: *16.5 millimeters.* **Weight:** *1.35 grams.* **Composition:** *89.24 percent silver (0.0388 troy ounces), 10.76 percent copper.*

	VG	VF		VG	VF
1796	1,550	4,700	1797 15 stars	1,500	4,650
1797 13 stars	2,650	5,800	1797 16 stars	1,750	4,900

Size: *16.5 millimeters.* **Weight:** *1.35 grams.* **Composition:** *89.24 percent silver (0.0388 troy ounces), 10.76 percent copper.*

	VG	VF
1800	1,250	2,350
1801	1,500	2,600
1802	65,000	135,000

	VG	VF
1803 large 8	1,375	2,475
1803 small 8	1,625	2,725
1805	1,525	2,825

LIBERTY CAP

Size: *15.5 millimeters.* **Weight:** *1.35 grams.* **Composition:** *89.24 percent silver (0.0388 troy ounces), 10.76 percent copper.*

	F	XF
1829	70.00	185
1830	60.00	155
1831	60.00	155
1832	60.00	155
1833	60.00	155
1834	60.00	155

	F	XF
1835	60.00	155
1835 large date, large 5C	75.00	170
1836	65.00	160
1837 large 5C	70.00	170
1837 small 5C	75.00	235

SEATED LIBERTY

No stars on obverse

Size: *15.5 millimeters.* **Weight:** *1.34 grams.* **Composition:** *90 percent silver (0.0388 troy ounces), 10 percent copper.*

	F	XF
1837 small date	75.00	220
1837 large date	80.00	235
1838-O	250	975

Stars on obverse

In 1840 drapery was added to Liberty's left elbow.

	F	XF			F	XF
1838 large stars	30.00	90.00		1842	25.00	55.00
1838 small stars	45.00	190		1842-O	75.00	550
1839	30.00	90.00		1843	25.00	55.00
1839-O	35.00	90.00		1844	25.00	60.00
1840 no drapery	30.00	80.00		1844-O	210	1,300
1840-O no drapery	40.00	140		1845	25.00	60.00
				1846	850	2,475
1840 with drapery	75.00	210		1847	25.00	55.00
1840-O	115	650		1848 medium date	25.00	65.00
1841	25.00	60.00		1848 large date	50.00	145
1841-O	30.00	125		1848-O	35.00	135

	F	XF
1849	30.00	65.00
1849-O	95.00	540
1850	25.00	60.00
1850-O	35.00	125
1851	25.00	55.00
1851-O	25.00	110

	F	XF
1852	25.00	55.00
1852-O	80.00	275
1853	90.00	300
1853-O	450	1,800

Arrows at date

Size: 15.5 millimeters. **Weight:** 1.24 grams. **Composition:** 90 percent silver (0.0362 troy ounces), 10 percent copper.

	F	XF
1853	25.00	60.00
1853-O	30.00	65.00
1854	25.00	60.00

	F	XF
1854-O	35.00	90.00
1855	25.00	60.00
1855-O	40.00	140

Arrows at date removed

Size: 15.5 millimeters. **Weight:** 1.24 grams. **Composition:** 90 percent silver (0.0362 troy ounces), 10 percent copper.

	F	XF
1856	25.00	50.00
1856-O	25.00	95.00
1857	25.00	50.00
1857-O	25.00	60.00

	F	XF
1858	25.00	50.00
1858-O	25.00	70.00
1859	25.00	55.00
1859-O	25.00	130

Obverse legend

	F	XF
1860	25.00	45.00
1860-O	25.00	50.00
1861	20.00	45.00
1862	35.00	65.00
1863	300	485
1863-S	70.00	165
1864	575	950
1864-S	115	250
1865	575	950
1865-S	60.00	145
1866	550	875
1866-S	60.00	145
1867	775	1,100
1867-S	60.00	150

	F	XF
1868	190	300
1868-S	35.00	60.00
1869	35.00	60.00
1869-S	30.00	55.00
1870	30.00	55.00
1870-S *one known*		
1871	20.00	45.00
1871-S	45.00	90.00
1872	20.00	45.00
1872-S	25.00	45.00
1873	20.00	45.00
1873-S	30.00	60.00

Nickel five cents

SHIELD

The Shield nickel was struck in the same composition as the nickel 3-cent, resulting in the first "nickel" 5-cent coin. The hard alloy was difficult to strike. As a result, fully struck examples in comparable grades command a premium.

Size: *20.5 millimeters.* **Weight:** *5 grams.* **Composition:** *75 percent copper, 25 percent nickel.* **Notes:** *In 1867 the rays between the stars on the reverse were eliminated, resulting in varieties with and without rays for that year.*

	F	XF
1866	55.00	150
1867 with rays	65.00	180
1867 without rays	30.00	65.00
1868	35.00	70.00
1869	30.00	65.00
1870	55.00	100
1871	140	310
1872	85.00	135
1873 open 3	55.00	80.00

	F	XF
1873 closed 3	70.00	150
1874	75.00	120
1875	90.00	170
1876	85.00	165
1877	—	proof 2,150
1878	—	proof 1,250
1879	625	720
1880	700	1,275
1881	430	600
1882	30.00	65.00
1883	30.00	70.00

LIBERTY

The Liberty nickel was originally struck with just a large Roman-numeral "V" on its reverse to indicate its value. At the time, some unscrupulous individuals gold plated the new nickels and passed them off as $5 coins. Thus, later in its first year of production, the word "Cents" was added to its reverse.

It is believed that the 1913 Liberty nickels were the unauthorized strikings of a U.S. Mint employee. Today, they are among numismatics' great rarities. All six known examples are accounted for in either private hands or museum holdings.

Size: *21.2 millimeters.* **Weight:** *5 grams.* **Composition:** *75 percent copper, 25 percent nickel.* **Notes:** *In 1883 the word "Cents" was added to the reverse, resulting in varieties with "Cents" and without "Cents" for that year.*

	F	XF
1883 without "Cents"	8.50	9.25
1883 with "Cents"	40.00	90.00
1884	40.00	90.00
1885	875	1,350
1886	400	685
1887	30.00	80.00
1888	70.00	185
1889	30.00	80.00
1890	25.00	70.00
1891	20.00	60.00
1892	25.00	65.00
1893	25.00	60.00
1894	100	230
1895	25.00	65.00
1896	40.00	100
1897	12.50	45.00
1898	10.00	40.00

	F	XF
1899	8.50	35.00
1900	8.50	35.00
1901	7.00	35.00
1902	4.00	30.00
1903	4.75	30.00
1904	4.75	30.00
1905	4.00	30.00
1906	4.00	30.00
1907	4.00	30.00
1908	4.00	30.00
1909	4.50	35.00
1910	4.00	30.00
1911	4.00	30.00
1912	4.00	30.00
1912-D	11.50	70.00
1912-S	220	810
1913 *6 known*		

BUFFALO

The Buffalo nickel, also and more appropriately called the Indian Head nickel, was a refreshing departure from previous coin designs. Noted sculptor James Earle Fraser designed the coin. It was long believed that three different Native Americans posed for the obverse portrait, but that theory has been questioned recently.

The original reverse, depicting an American bison standing on a mound, was changed because the words "Five Cents" were in such high relief that they wore off quickly. The second reverse has the denomination in a recess below a plane on which the bison stands. The date is also in high relief and, as a result, is usually worn off on coins grading below very good. "Dateless" Buffalo nickels have little value.

Size: *21.2 millimeters.* **Weight:** *5 grams.* **Composition:** *75 percent copper, 25 percent nickel.* **Notes:** *In 1913 the reverse design was modified so the ground under the buffalo was represented as a line rather than a mound. On the 1937-D "three-legged" variety, the buffalo's right front leg is missing, the result of a damaged die.*

	F	MS-60
1913 mound	15.00	35.00
1913-D mound	20.00	65.00
1913-S mound	50.00	125
1913 line	13.00	35.00
1913-D line	180	285
1913-S line	420	885
1914	20.00	45.00
1914-D	165	475
1914-S	45.00	165
1915	7.75	50.00

	F	MS-60
1915-D	40.00	235
1915-S	100	625
1916	7.00	45.00
1916-D	30.00	165
1916-S	25.00	185
1917	8.75	60.00
1917-D	55.00	345
1917-S	80.00	400
1918	8.00	100
1918-D	65.00	430
1918-S	55.00	500

	F	MS-60
1919	4.00	60.00
1919-D	65.00	570
1919-S	50.00	540
1920	3.25	60.00
1920-D	35.00	575
1920-S	30.00	525
1921	8.50	125
1921-S	180	1,575
1923	4.25	60.00
1923-S	25.00	625
1924	4.50	75.00
1924-D	30.00	375
1924-S	95.00	2,300
1925	3.75	40.00
1925-D	40.00	375
1925-S	17.50	425
1926	3.00	30.00
1926-D	30.00	335
1926-S	100	4,950
1927	2.50	35.00
1927-D	7.00	155
1927-S	6.00	490
1928	2.50	30.00

	F	MS-60
1928-D	3.75	55.00
1928-S	3.00	225
1929	2.50	35.00
1929-D	3.00	60.00
1929-S	2.25	50.00
1930	2.50	35.00
1930-S	3.00	65.00
1931-S	17.00	60.00
1934	2.50	45.00
1934-D	4.75	80.00
1935	2.25	20.00
1935-D	3.00	70.00
1935-S	2.50	50.00
1936	2.25	14.50
1936-D	2.75	35.00
1936-S	2.50	35.00
1937	2.25	14.50
1937-D	2.50	30.00
1937-D three-legged	725	2,375
1937-S	2.50	25.00
1938-D	4.00	25.00

JEFFERSON

The Jefferson nickel was the first circulating U.S. coin to be designed by public contest. Felix Schlag won $1,000 for his design featuring Thomas Jefferson on the obverse and his home, Monticello, on the reverse. Schlag's initials were added to the design in 1966.

The steps leading up to Monticello on the reverse are a key to evaluating the coin. They don't always strike up completely, so Jefferson nickels with fully struck steps command a premium.

During World War II, nickel was needed for the war effort, so from mid-1942 through 1945, "nickels" were struck in an unusual alloy of 56 percent copper, 35 percent silver, and 9 percent manganese. The "war nickels" have a large mintmark over the dome of Monticello on the reverse.

Congress authorized new nickel designs for 2004 and 2005 to commemorate the bicentennial of Lewis and Clark's exploration of the American West following the Louisiana Purchase. As president, Jefferson authorized the mission to find the "most direct and practicable water communication across this continent for the purpose of commerce." For 2006, an image of Jefferson based on a Rembrandt Peale portrait from 1800 was used on the obverse.

Size: *21.2 millimeters.* **Weight:** *5 grams.* **Composition:** *75 percent copper, 25 percent nickel.*

	F	MS-60
1938	0.75	7.50
1938-D	1.25	4.00
1938-S	2.00	5.25
1939	0.20	1.75
1939-D	5.00	55.00
1939-S	0.60	17.00
1940	0.20	1.00

	F	MS-60
1940-D	0.20	1.50
1940-S	0.40	4.50
1941	—	0.75
1941-D	0.30	2.25
1941-S	0.40	5.00
1942	—	5.00
1942-D	3.00	40.00

Wartime composition

Composition: *56 percent copper, 25 percent silver (0.0563 troy ounces), 9 percent manganese.* **Notes:** *The mintmark on wartime-composition nickels appears above the dome of Monticello on the reverse.*

	VF	MS-60
1942-P	2.50	9.00
1942-S	2.50	11.00
1943-P	2.50	5.00
1943-D	3.00	4.00
1943-S	2.50	6.75
1944-P	2.50	14.00

	VF	MS-60
1944-D	2.75	12.00
1944-S	2.75	9.50
1945-P	2.75	6.00
1945-D	2.75	5.50
1945-S	2.75	5.00

Pre-war composition resumed

	XF	MS-65		XF	MS-65
1946	0.25	20.00	1956	0.15	16.00
1946-D	0.35	16.00	1956-D	0.15	16.00
1946-S	0.40	17.00	1957	0.15	12.00
1947	0.25	18.00	1957-D	0.15	12.00
1947-D	0.30	15.00	1958	0.20	30.00
1947-S	0.25	15.00	1958-D	0.15	13.00
1948	0.25	16.00	1959	—	8.00
1948-D	0.35	14.00	1959-D	—	5.50
1948-S	0.50	14.00	1960	—	6.00
1949	0.30	18.00	1960-D	—	20.00
1949-D	0.40	12.00	1961	—	6.00
1949-S	1.00	10.00	1961-D	—	20.00
1950	0.75	12.00	1962	—	5.00
1950-D	10.00	20.00	1962-D	—	0.75
1951	0.50	18.00	1963	—	0.55
1951-D	0.50	14.00	1963-D	—	0.55
1951-S	1.00	18.50	1964	—	0.55
1952	0.25	17.00	1964-D	—	0.50
1952-D	0.50	18.00	1965	—	0.50
1952-S	0.25	18.00	1966	—	0.50
1953	0.25	9.00	1967	—	0.50
1953-D	0.25	16.00	1968-D	—	4.50
1953-S	0.25	20.00	1968-S	—	0.50
1954	0.20	9.00	1969-D	—	0.50
1954-D	0.20	10.00	1969-S	—	0.50
1954-S	0.20	16.00	1970-D	—	0.50
1955	0.45	6.50	1970-S	—	8.00
1955-D	0.15	16.00	1971	—	2.00

	XF	MS-65		XF	MS-65
1971-D	—	0.50	1981-P	—	0.40
1971-S		proof 2.00	1981-D	—	0.40
1972	—	0.50	1981-S	—	proof 2.00
1972-D	—	0.50	1982-P	—	12.50
1972-S		proof 2.00	1982-D	—	3.50
1973		0.50	1982-S	—	proof 3.50
1973-D	—	0.50	1983-P	—	4.00
1973-S		proof 1.75	1983-D	—	2.50
1974	—	0.50	1983-S	—	proof 4.00
1974-D	—	0.50	1984-P	—	3.00
1974-S		proof 2.00	1984-D	—	0.85
1975	—	0.75	1984-S	—	proof 5.00
1975-D	—	0.50	1985-P	—	0.75
1975-S	—	proof 2.25	1985-D	—	0.75
1976	—	0.75	1985-S	—	proof 4.00
1976-D		0.60	1986-P	—	1.00
1976-S	—	proof 3.00	1986-D	—	2.00
1977	—	0.40	1986-S	—	proof 7.00
1977-D	—	0.55	1987-P	—	0.75
1977-S	—	proof 1.75	1987-D	—	0.75
1978	—	0.40	1987-S	—	proof 3.50
1978-D	—	0.40	1988-P	—	0.75
1978-S	—	proof 1.75	1988-D	—	0.75
1979	—	0.40	1988-S	—	proof 6.50
1979-D	—	0.40	1988-P	—	0.75
1979-S	—	proof 1.50	1989-D	—	0.75
1980-P	—	6.00	1989-S	—	proof 5.50
1980-D	—	0.40	1990-P	—	0.75
1980-S	—	proof 1.50	1990-D	—	0.75

	XF	MS-65		XF	MS-65
1990-S	—	*proof* 5.50	1997-D	—	2.00
1991-P	—	0.75	1997-S		*proof* 5.00
1991-D	—	0.75	1998-P	—	0.80
1991-S	—	*proof* 5.00	1998-D	—	0.80
1992-P	—	2.00	1998-S		*proof* 4.50
1992-D	—	0.75	1999-P	—	0.80
1992-S	—	*proof* 4.00	1999-D	—	0.80
1993-P	—	0.75	1999-S		*proof* 3.50
1993-D	—	0.75	2000-P	—	0.80
1993-S	—	*proof* 4.50	2000-D	—	0.80
1994-P	—	0.75	2000-S		*proof* 2.00
1994-D	—	0.75	2001-P	—	0.50
1994-S	—	*proof* 4.00	2001-D	—	0.50
1995-P	—	0.75	2001-S		*proof* 4.00
1995-D	—	0.85	2002-P	—	0.50
1995-S	—	*proof* 4.00	2002-D	—	0.50
1996-P	—	0.75	2002-S		*proof* 2.00
1996-D	—	0.75	2003-P	—	0.50
1996-S	—	*proof* 4.00	2003-D	—	0.50
1997-P	—	0.75	2003-S		*proof* 2.00

WESTWARD JOURNEY NICKELS

Peace medal

	MS-65	PF-65
2004-P	1.50	—
2004-D	1.50	—
2004-S	—	10.00

Bison

	MS-65	PF-65
2005-P	1.50	—
2005-D	1.50	—
2005-S	—	6.50

Keelboat

	MS-65	PF-65
2004-P	1.50	—
2004-D	1.50	—
2004-S	—	10.00

"Ocean in view!"

	MS-65	PF-65
2005-P	1.25	—
2005-D	1.25	—
2005-S	—	5.50

NEW JEFFERSON PORTRAIT

	MS-65	PF-65
2006-P	2.50	—
2006-P satin finish	4.00	—
2006-D	2.50	—
2006-D satin finish	4.00	—
2006-S	—	5.00
2007-P	2.50	—
2007-P satin finish	4.00	—
2007-D	2.50	—
2007-D satin finish	4.00	—
2007-S	—	4.00
2008-P	2.50	—
2008-P satin finish	4.00	—
2008-D	2.50	—
2008-D satin finish	4.00	—

	MS-65	PF-65
2008-S	—	4.00
2009-P	2.50	—
2009-P satin finish	4.00	—
2009-D	2.50	—
2009-D satin finish	4.00	—
2009-S	—	3.00
2010-P	2.50	—
2010-P satin finish	4.00	—
2010-D	2.50	—
2010-D satin finish	4.00	—
2010-S	—	3.00
2011-P	2.50	—
2011-D	2.50	—
2011-S	—	3.00

Dimes

DRAPED BUST

The dime was among the denominations originally authorized in 1792, but production did not begin until 1796 as the fledgling U.S. Mint concentrated initially on the lower denominations. In 1798, the rather scrawny eagle on the reverse was replaced by a more dignified heraldic eagle.

Small eagle

Size: *19 millimeters.* **Weight:** *2.7 grams.*
Composition: *89.24 percent silver (0.0775 troy ounces), 10.76 percent copper.*

	VG	VF
1796	3,465	5,350
1797 13 stars	3,615	5,600

	VG	VF
1797 16 stars	3,490	5,425

Heraldic eagle

	VG	VF
1798	1,250	1,850
1800	1,075	2,550
1801	1,150	2,750
1802	2,650	4,750
1803	1,150	2,750

	VG	VF
1804 13 stars	4,450	19,000
1804 14 stars	6,500	24,500
1805	1,000	1,950
1807	900	1,500

LIBERTY CAP

A design revision in 1809 saw Liberty turned around – from facing the viewer's right to facing the viewer's left – and a cap added to her head. The denomination – designated as "10C" – was also added to the coin for the first time as part of the reverse design revision.

Size: *18.8 millimeters (1809-1828) and 18.5 millimeters (1828-1837).* **Weight:** *2.7 grams.*
Composition: *89.24 percent silver (0.0775 troy ounces), 10.76 percent copper.*

	VG	VF
1809	220	700
1811	175	650
1814 small date	80.00	300
1814 large date	50.00	135
1820	50.00	125
1821	50.00	130
1822	1,850	4,500
1823	50.00	130
1824	80.00	300
1825	45.00	110
1827	45.00	110

	VG	VF
1828	110	375
1828 smaller size	50.00	155
1829	40.00	90.00
1830	40.00	85.00
1831	40.00	85.00
1832	40.00	85.00
1833	40.00	85.00
1834	40.00	85.00
1835	40.00	85.00
1836	40.00	85.00
1837	40.00	90.00

SEATED LIBERTY

Christian Gobrecht's Seated Liberty design first appeared on the dollar and was later adapted for the lower denominations. The Seated Liberty dime underwent a number of modifications in design and specifications during its long run, as noted in the listings that follow. In some cases, a design tweak indicated a change in specifications.

No stars on obverse

Size: 17.9 millimeters. **Weight:** 2.67 grams.
Composition: 90 percent silver (0.0773 troy ounces), 10 percent copper.

	VG	VF
1837	50.00	290

	VG	VF
1838-O	60.00	375

In 1840 drapery was added to Liberty's left elbow.

	VG	VF
1838 small stars	30.00	80.00
1838 large stars	20.00	35.00
1839	18.50	35.00
1839-O	20.00	60.00
1840 no drapery	18.50	35.00
1840-O no drapery	25.00	70.00
1840 with drapery	50.00	185
1841	18.50	30.00
1841-O	25.00	45.00
1842	17.50	25.00
1842-O	25.00	75.00
1843	17.50	25.00
1843-O	80.00	325

	VG	VF
1844	350	800
1845	18.50	30.00
1845-O	35.00	250
1846	350	950
1847	25.00	85.00
1848	20.00	50.00
1849	20.00	35.00
1849-O	30.00	135
1850	20.00	35.00
1850-O	25.00	90.00
1851	20.00	30.00
1851-O	25.00	90.00
1852	15.00	25.00
1852-O	30.00	125
1853	125	300

Arrows at date

Size: *17.9 millimeters.* **Weight:** *2.49 grams.* **Composition:** *90 percent silver (0.0721 troy ounces), 10 percent copper.*

	VG	VF
1853	9.00	14.00
1853-O	14.00	45.00
1854	9.25	15.00

	VG	VF
1854-O	11.00	25.00
1855	9.25	20.00

Arrows at date removed

	VG	VF
1856	15.00	25.00
1856-O	18.50	35.00
1856-S	225	550
1857	15.50	25.00
1857-O	16.00	30.00
1858	15.00	25.00

	VG	VF
1858-O	25.00	85.00
1858-S	200	475
1859	20.00	45.00
1859-O	20.00	45.00
1859-S	225	550
1860-S	55.00	145

	VG	VF		VG	VF
1860	20.00	30.00	1868	20.00	40.00
1860-O	600	1,950	1868-S	35.00	85.00
1861	17.00	25.00	1869	35.00	80.00
1861-S	90.00	275	1869-S	30.00	55.00
1862	17.50	25.00	1870	20.00	40.00
1862-S	65.00	185	1870-S	375	650
1863	500	900	1871	20.00	35.00
1863-S	55.00	145	1871-CC	3,500	6,500
1864	500	750	1871-S	55.00	130
1864-S	45.00	110	1872	15.00	20.00
1865	575	875	1872-S	65.00	150
1865-S	55.00	145	1872-CC	1,250	3,000
1866	600	950	1873 closed 3	15.00	20.00
1866-S	65.00	150	1873 open 3	35.00	75.00
1867	700	1,100	1873-CC *rare*		
1867-S	60.00	150			

Arrows at date

Size: *17.9 millimeters.* **Weight:** *2.5 grams.*
Composition: *90 percent silver (0.0724 troy ounces), 10 percent copper.*

	VG	VF
1873	18.50	55.00
1873-CC	3,250	6,500
1873-S	30.00	70.00

	VG	VF
1874	17.50	50.00
1874-CC	6,500	12,500
1874-S	75.00	160

Arrows at date removed

	VG	VF
1875	16.00	20.00
1875-CC	20.00	40.00
1875-S mintmark in wreath	25.00	45.00
1875-S mintmark under wreath	15.00	20.00
1876	20.00	30.00
1876-CC	30.00	50.00
1876-S	16.00	25.00
1877	16.00	25.00
1877-CC	30.00	50.00
1877-S	18.00	30.00

	VG	VF
1878	20.00	50.00
1878-CC	100	250
1879	310	425
1880	275	350
1881	300	400
1882	16.00	20.00
1883	16.00	20.00
1884	16.00	20.00
1884-S	35.00	55.00
1885	16.00	20.00
1885-S	650	1,750
1886	15.00	20.00

	VG	VF
1886-S	70.00	125
1887	16.00	20.00
1887-S	15.00	20.00
1888	16.00	20.00
1888-S	15.00	25.00
1889	16.00	20.00

	VG	VF
1889-S	18.00	45.00
1890	16.00	20.00
1890-S	15.00	50.00
1891	16.00	20.00
1891-O	15.00	20.00
1891-S	15.00	20.00

BARBER

The dime, quarter, and half dollar were all revised in 1892 to depict a right-facing portrait of Liberty designed by U.S. Mint Chief Engraver Charles Barber, for whom they have been popularly named.

Size: *17.9 millimeters.* **Weight:** *2.5 grams.*
Composition: *90 percent silver (0.0724 troy ounces), 10 percent copper.*

	F	XF
1892	16.00	30.00
1892-O	35.00	75.00
1892-S	210	285
1893	20.00	45.00
1893-O	135	190
1893-S	40.00	85.00
1894	125	190
1894-O	215	425
1894-S *rare*		

	F	XF
1895	355	565
1895-O	900	2,500
1895-S	135	240
1896	55.00	100
1896-O	300	465
1896-S	310	385
1897	8.00	30.00
1897-O	290	480
1897-S	100	185

	F	XF
1898	7.50	30.00
1898-O	90.00	200
1898-S	35.00	80.00
1899	7.50	25.00
1899-O	75.00	150
1899-S	35.00	45.00
1900	7.00	25.00
1900-O	115	225
1900-S	12.50	30.00
1901	6.50	30.00
1901-O	16.00	70.00
1901-S	360	520
1902	6.25	25.00
1902-O	15.00	65.00
1902-S	60.00	135
1903	6.25	25.00
1903-O	13.50	50.00
1903-S	350	750
1904	7.00	25.00
1904-S	165	335
1905	6.75	25.00
1905-O	35.00	90.00
1905-S	9.00	45.00
1906	4.50	20.00
1906-D	7.00	35.00
1906-O	50.00	100
1906-S	12.50	45.00
1907	4.25	20.00
1907-D	8.75	45.00

	F	XF
1907-O	35.00	65.00
1907-S	16.00	65.00
1908	4.25	20.00
1908-D	5.75	30.00
1908-O	45.00	90.00
1908-S	11.50	45.00
1909	4.25	20.00
1909-D	60.00	135
1909-O	12.50	50.00
1909-S	90.00	180
1910	4.00	20.00
1910-D	8.50	50.00
1910-S	50.00	110
1911	4.00	20.00
1911-D	4.00	20.00
1911-S	8.50	40.00
1912	4.00	20.00
1912-D	4.00	20.00
1912-S	6.00	35.00
1913	4.00	20.00
1913-S	120	240
1914	4.00	20.00
1914-D	4.00	20.00
1914-S	8.00	40.00
1915	4.00	20.00
1915-S	35.00	65.00
1916	4.00	20.00
1916-S	5.00	25.00

MERCURY

The common name Mercury for this dime is a misnomer. Designed by Adolph Weinman, it actually depicts Liberty wearing a winged cap, representing freedom of thought, rather than the Roman god Mercury. The reverse depicts the ancient Roman fasces, a symbol of authority that is part of the U.S. Senate's official seal.

The horizontal bands tying the fasces together do not always strike up distinctly from each other. Mercury dimes with "fully split bands" often command a premium.

Size: *17.9 millimeters.* **Weight:** *2.5 grams.*
Composition: *90 percent silver (0.0724 troy ounces), 10 percent copper.*

	VF	MS-60		VF	MS-60
1916	7.00	30.00	1919-S	20.00	175
1916-D	3,850	13,750	1920	4.50	30.00
1916-S	15.00	45.00	1920-D	9.00	110
1917	5.50	30.00	1920-S	9.00	110
1917-D	25.00	120	1921	260	1,175
1917-S	7.50	60.00	1921-D	380	1,300
1918	12.00	70.00	1923	3.50	30.00
1918-D	13.00	100	1923-S	20.00	155
1918-S	11.00	95.00	1924	4.50	40.00
1919	5.50	35.00	1924-D	25.00	165
1919-D	30.00	175	1924-S	12.00	185

	VF	MS-60
1925	5.50	30.00
1925-D	45.00	335
1925-S	18.50	180
1926	3.50	25.00
1926-D	12.00	125
1926-S	65.00	850
1927	3.50	25.00
1927-D	25.00	165
1927-S	11.00	270
1928	3.50	30.00
1928-D	25.00	165
1928-S	6.50	140
1929	3.50	20.00
1929-D	8.00	30.00
1929-S	5.00	35.00
1930	3.50	25.00
1930-S	6.50	80.00
1931	4.75	35.00
1931-D	20.00	100
1931-S	11.00	100.00
1934	3.50	30.00
1934-D	7.50	50.00
1935	3.50	10.00
1935-D	6.50	40.00
1935-S	4.25	25.00
1936	3.50	9.00
1936-D	4.25	30.00
1936-S	4.00	20.00
1937	3.50	8.00

	VF	MS-60
1937-D	4.00	20.00
1937-S	4.00	20.00
1938	3.50	13.50
1938-D	5.00	18.50
1938-S	4.00	20.00
1939	3.50	9.00
1939-D	3.50	7.50
1939-S	4.00	25.00
1940	3.50	6.00
1940-D	3.50	8.00
1940-S	3.50	8.50
1941	3.50	6.00
1941-D	3.50	8.00
1941-S	3.50	7.00
1942	3.50	6.00
1942-D	3.50	8.00
1942-S	3.50	10.00
1943	3.50	6.00
1943-D	3.50	8.00
1943-S	3.50	9.50
1944	3.50	6.00
1944-D	3.50	7.50
1944-S	3.50	7.50
1945	3.50	6.00
1945-D	3.50	6.50
1945-S	3.50	7.00

ROOSEVELT

The Roosevelt dime was introduced as a tribute to the late President Franklin D. Roosevelt and was designed by U.S. Mint Chief Engraver John R. Sinnock. Calls for Roosevelt to be honored on a coin came soon after his death on April 12, 1945. Congressional approval is required to change any coin design that has been used for less than 25 years. At the time of Roosevelt's death, the Lincoln cent, Mercury dime, and Walking Liberty half dollar were eligible for redesign. The dime was chosen because the March of Dimes was a fund-raising campaign for the National Foundation for Infantile Paralysis, which Roosevelt established in 1938. Roosevelt suffered from the disease, commonly called polio.

Size: *17.9 millimeters.* **Weight:** *2.5 grams.*
Composition: *90 percent silver (0.0724 troy ounces), 10 percent copper.*

	MS-60	MS-65
1946	4.00	14.50
1946-D	4.00	13.50
1946-S	4.00	18.50
1947	3.75	15.00
1947-D	4.50	16.00
1947-S	3.75	15.00
1948	3.75	14.00
1948-D	5.00	15.00
1948-S	4.50	17.00
1949	16.00	65.00
1949-D	9.00	25.00

	MS-60	MS-65
1949-S	35.00	65.00
1950	7.00	30.00
1950-D	3.75	15.00
1950-S	25.00	70.00
1951	4.00	11.00
1951-D	4.00	11.00
1951-S	10.00	35.00
1952	4.00	20.00
1952-D	4.00	11.00
1952-S	5.50	16.00
1953	4.00	12.00

	MS-60	MS-65
1953-D	4.25	11.00
1953-S	5.50	12.50
1954	4.00	10.00
1954-D	4.00	10.00
1954-S	4.00	10.00
1955	4.00	8.50
1955-D	4.00	8.50
1955-S	4.00	8.00
1956	4.00	9.50
1956-D	4.00	9.00
1957	4.00	8.50
1957-D	4.00	7.50
1958	4.00	11.00

	MS-60	MS-65
1958-D	4.00	10.00
1959	4.00	8.00
1959-D	4.00	8.50
1960	3.50	8.50
1960-D	4.00	7.50
1961	4.00	8.00
1961-D	4.00	6.50
1962	4.00	6.50
1962-D	4.00	7.00
1963	4.00	7.50
1963-D	4.00	7.00
1964	4.00	7.50
1964-D	4.00	7.00

Clad composition

Size: 17.9 millimeters. **Weight:** 2.27 grams. **Composition:** Clad layers of 75 percent copper and 25 percent nickel bonded to a pure copper core. **Notes:** Starting in 1992, Roosevelt dimes in the traditional 90 percent silver composition were struck for inclusion in silver proof sets, which also included silver quarters and silver half dollars.

	MS-65	PF-65			MS-65	PF-65
1965	1.00	—		1975	1.00	—
1966	1.00	—		1975-D	1.00	—
1967	1.50	—		1975-S	—	2.00
1968	1.00	—		1976	1.50	—
1968-D	1.00	—		1976-D	1.00	—
1968-S	—	1.00		1976-S	—	1.00
1969	3.00	—		1977	1.00	—
1969-D	1.00	—		1977-D	1.00	—
1969-S	—	0.80		1977-S	—	2.00
1970	1.00	—		1978	1.00	—
1970-D	1.00	—		1978-D	1.00	—
1970-S	—	1.00		1978-S	—	1.00
1971	2.00	—		1979	1.00	—
1971-D	1.00	—		1979-D	1.00	—
1971-S	—	1.00		1979-S	—	1.00
1972	1.00	—		1980-P	1.00	—
1972-D	1.00	—		1980-D	0.70	—
1972-S	—	1.00		1980-S	—	1.00
1973	1.00	—		1981-P	1.00	—
1973-D	1.00	—		1981-D	1.00	—
1973-S	—	1.00		1981-S	—	1.00
1974	1.00	—		1982-P	8.50	—
1974-D	1.00	—		1982-D	3.00	—
1974-S	—	1.00		1982-S	—	2.00

	MS-65	PF-65
1983-P	7.00	—
1983-D	2.50	—
1983-S	—	2.00
1984-P	1.00	—
1984-D	2.00	—
1984-S	—	2.00
1985-P	1.00	—
1985-D	1.00	—
1985-S	—	1.00
1986-P	2.00	—
1986-D	2.00	—
1986-S	—	2.75
1987-P	1.00	—
1987-D	1.00	—
1987-S	—	1.00
1988-P	1.00	—
1988-D	1.00	—
1988-S	—	3.00
1989-P	1.00	—
1989-D	1.00	—
1989-S	—	4.00
1990-P	1.00	—
1990-D	1.00	—
1990-S	—	2.00
1991-P	1.00	—
1991-D	1.00	—
1991-S	—	3.00
1992-P	1.00	—
1992-D	1.00	—

	MS-65	PF-65
1992-S	—	4.00
1992-S silver	—	5.00
1993-P	1.00	—
1993-D	1.50	—
1993-S	—	7.00
1993-S silver	—	9.00
1994-P	1.00	—
1994-D	1.00	—
1994-S	—	5.00
1994-S silver	—	9.00
1995-P	1.50	—
1995-D	2.00	—
1995-S	—	20.00
1995-S silver	—	25.00
1996-P	1.00	—
1996-D	1.00	—
1996-W	25.00	—
1996-S	—	2.50
1996-S silver	—	9.00
1997-P	2.00	—
1997-D	1.00	—
1997-S	—	11.00
1997-S silver	—	25.00
1998-P	1.00	—
1998-D	1.25	—
1998-S	—	4.00
1998-S silver	—	9.00
1999-P	1.00	—
1999-D	1.00	—

	MS-65	PF-65
1999-S	—	4.00
1999-S silver	—	6.50
2000-P	1.00	—
2000-D	1.00	—
2000-S	—	1.00
2000-S silver	—	4.00
2001-P	1.00	—
2001-D	1.00	—
2001-S	—	1.00
2001-S silver	—	5.00
2002-P	1.00	—
2002-D	1.00	—
2002-S	—	1.00
2002-S silver	—	5.00
2003-P	1.00	—
2003-D	1.00	—
2003-S	—	1.00
2003-S silver	—	4.00
2004-P	1.00	—
2004-D	1.00	—
2004-S	—	4.75
2004-S silver	—	4.50
2005-P	1.00	—
2005-D	1.00	—
2005-S	—	2.25

	MS-65	PF-65
2005-S silver	—	3.50
2006-P	1.00	—
2006-D	1.00	—
2006-S	—	2.25
2006-S silver	—	3.50
2007-P	1.00	—
2007-D	1.00	—
2007-S	—	2.25
2007-S silver	—	3.50
2008-P	1.00	—
2008-D	1.00	—
2008-S	—	2.25
2008-S silver	—	3.50
2009-P	1.00	—
2009-D	1.00	—
2009-S	—	2.25
2009-S silver	—	3.50
2010-P	1.00	—
2010-D	1.00	—
2010-S	—	2.25
2010-S silver	—	3.50
2011-P	1.00	—
2011-D	1.00	—
2011-S	—	2.25
2011-S silver	—	3.50

Twenty cents

When designing the 20-cent piece, U.S. Mint officials were concerned that the public would confuse it with the quarter because of the similarity in size. To give it a distinctive look, the eagle on the reverse faces to its left rather than its right, as on the quarter; the word "Liberty" on the obverse shield is in relief rather than incuse; and the 20-cent coin's edge is plain rather than reeded. The changes weren't enough, however, and circulation production of the coin ended after only two years.

Most of the 1876-CC circulation-production coins were not released and were melted by the Mint. Only one is known to exist today. Only collector proofs were struck in 1877 and 1878.

Size: *22 millimeters.* **Weight:** *5 grams.*
Composition: *90 percent silver (0.1447 troy ounces), 10 percent copper.*

	VG	VF
1875	210	325
1875-S	110	175
1875-CC	385	600
1876	225	350

	VG	VF
1876-CC		*proof* 60,000
1877		*proof* 3,500
1878		*proof* 2,800

Quarters

DRAPED BUST

The quarter was among the denominations originally authorized in 1792, but production did not begin until 1796 as the fledgling U.S. Mint concentrated initially on the lower denominations. After its first year, quarter production did not resume until 1804, when the rather scrawny eagle on the reverse was replaced by a more dignified heraldic eagle. The denomination – designated as "25C" – was also added to the coin for the first time in 1804.

Small eagle

Size: *27.5 millimeters.* **Weight:** *6.74 grams.*
Composition: *89.24 percent silver (0.1935 troy ounces), 10.76 percent copper.*

	VG	VF
1796	16,500	39,500

Heraldic eagle

	VG	VF
1804	6,750	14,500
1805	285	960
1806	275	900
1807	275	925

LIBERTY CAP

After another break in production, the U.S. Mint resumed issuing quarters in 1812. The new design saw Liberty turned around – from facing the viewer's right to facing the viewer's left – and a cap added to her head.

Reverse motto

Size: *27 millimeters.* **Weight:** *6.74 grams.* **Composition:** *89.24 percent silver (0.1935 troy ounces), 10.76 percent copper.*

	VG	VF
1815	135	425
1818	125	410
1819	125	410
1820	125	415
1821	130	420
1822	135	440

	VG	VF
1823	35,000	58,500
1824	425	1,650
1825	150	450
1827	—	70,000
1828	120	400

Reverse motto removed

Size: *24.3 millimeters.* **Notes:** *In 1831 the motto "E Pluribus Unum" was removed from the reverse.*

	VG	VF
1831	90.00	150
1832	90.00	150
1833	100	170
1834	90.00	150

	VG	VF
1835	90.00	150
1836	90.00	150
1837	90.00	150
1838	90.00	150

Christian Gobrecht's Seated Liberty design first appeared on the dollar and was later adapted for the lower denominations. The Seated Liberty quarter underwent a number of modifications in design and specifications during its long run, as noted in the listings that follow. In some cases, a design tweak indicated a change in specifications.

Size: *24.3 millimeters.* **Weight:** *6.68 grams.* **Composition:** *90 percent silver (0.1934 troy ounces), 10 percent copper.* **Notes:** *In 1840 drapery was added to Liberty's left elbow.*

	VG	VF
1838	45.00	95.00
1839	45.00	90.00
1840-O no drapery	55.00	135
1840 with drapery	40.00	110
1840-O with drapery	40.00	115
1841	90.00	170
1841-O	30.00	85.00
1842	125	275
1842-O small date	650	1,950
1842-O large date	45.00	70.00
1843	30.00	45.00
1843-O	45.00	125

	VG	VF
1844	30.00	45.00
1844-O	45.00	75.00
1845	30.00	45.00
1846	35.00	45.00
1847	30.00	50.00
1847-O	45.00	135
1848	60.00	185
1849	35.00	65.00
1849-O	750	1,850
1850	50.00	125
1850-O	45.00	110
1851	75.00	225
1851-O	275	700
1852	60.00	185
1852-O	275	800

Arrows at date, reverse rays

Size: *24.3 millimeters.* **Weight:** *6.22 grams.*
Composition: *90 percent silver (0.18 troy ounces), 10 percent copper.*

	VG	VF
1853	30.00	45.00
1853-O	45.00	85.00

Reverse rays removed

	VG	VF
1854	30.00	40.00
1854-O	35.00	60.00
1855	30.00	40.00
1855-O	75.00	240
1855-S	60.00	225

Arrows at date removed

	VG	VF
1856	30.00	45.00
1856-O	35.00	60.00
1856-S	65.00	250
1857	30.00	45.00
1857-O	35.00	45.00
1857-S	175	450
1858	30.00	45.00
1858-O	35.00	70.00
1858-S	110	300
1859	35.00	45.00
1859-O	30.00	80.00
1859-S	150	500

	VG	VF
1860	35.00	50.00
1860-O	30.00	55.00
1860-S	350	975
1861	20.00	35.00
1861-S	145	400
1862	25.00	40.00
1862-S	125	325
1863	60.00	140
1864	120	245
1864-S	600	1,350
1865	115	235
1865-S	175	425

"In God We Trust" above eagle

	VG	VF
1866	600	1,000
1866-S	375	1,050
1867	325	675
1867-S	385	900
1868	250	400
1868-S	110	300
1869	450	800
1869-S	135	375
1870	80.00	245
1870-CC	10,000	24,500

	VG	VF
1871	65.00	150
1871-CC	4,500	12,500
1871-S	500	950
1872	40.00	110
1872-CC	1,500	3,750
1872-S	1,250	2,400
1873 closed 3	350	800
1873 open 3	45.00	120
1873-CC *six known*		

Arrows at date

Size: *24.3 millimeters.* **Weight:** *6.25 grams.*
Composition: *90 percent silver (0.1809 troy ounces), 10 percent copper.*

	VG	VF
1873	30.00	60.00
1873-CC	4,500	11,000
1873-S	40.00	140

	VG	VF
1874	30.00	60.00
1874-S	35.00	110

	VG	VF
1875	30.00	40.00
1875-CC	110	350
1875-S	35.00	110
1876	30.00	40.00
1876-CC	70.00	100
1876-S	30.00	40.00
1877	30.00	40.00
1877-CC	70.00	100
1877-S	30.00	40.00
1878	30.00	40.00
1878-CC	75.00	125
1878-S	200	400
1879	235	325
1880	235	325

	VG	VF
1881	250	350
1882	250	350
1883	265	365
1884	450	650
1885	265	365
1886	600	800
1887	350	550
1888	325	500
1888-S	30.00	40.00
1889	300	425
1890	85.00	125
1891	30.00	40.00
1891-O	225	550
1891-S	30.00	45.00

BARBER

The dime, quarter, and half dollar were all revised in 1892 to depict a right-facing portrait of Liberty designed by U.S. Mint Chief Engraver Charles Barber, for whom they have been popularly named.

Size: *24.3 millimeters.* **Weight:** *6.25 grams.* **Composition:** *90 percent silver (0.1809 troy ounces), 10 percent copper.*

	F	XF
1892	35.00	100
1892-O	55.00	155
1892-S	135	300
1893	30.00	70.00
1893-O	45.00	165
1893-S	80.00	255
1894	35.00	95.00
1894-O	50.00	165
1894-S	50.00	180
1895	30.00	80.00
1895-O	60.00	175
1895-S	85.00	235
1896	25.00	80.00
1896-O	125	435
1896-S	2,350	4,650

	F	XF
1897	20.00	70.00
1897-O	130	400
1897-S	235	440
1898	25.00	75.00
1898-O	75.00	300
1898-S	50.00	100
1899	25.00	75.00
1899-O	40.00	145
1899-S	70.00	145
1900	25.00	70.00
1900-O	70.00	170
1900-S	40.00	80.00
1901	25.00	80.00
1901-O	145	455
1901-S	17,500	30,000

	F	XF
1902	20.00	65.00
1902-O	50.00	150
1902-S	55.00	170
1903	20.00	60.00
1903-O	40.00	125
1903-S	45.00	145
1904	20.00	70.00
1904-D	65.00	225
1905	30.00	70.00
1905-O	85.00	265
1905-S	45.00	110
1906	18.50	65.00
1906-D	25.00	70.00
1906-O	40.00	110
1907	16.50	60.00
1907-D	30.00	80.00
1907-O	20.00	65.00
1907-S	50.00	135
1908	18.50	65.00
1908-D	17.50	65.00
1908-O	17.50	70.00
1908-S	90.00	300

	F	XF
1909	17.50	65.00
1909-D	20.00	90.00
1909-O	95.00	375
1909-S	35.00	95.00
1910	30.00	80.00
1910-D	50.00	130
1911	20.00	70.00
1911-D	95.00	330
1911-S	50.00	180
1912	17.50	70.00
1912-S	45.00	130
1913	75.00	390
1913-D	40.00	95.00
1913-S	5,000	10,500
1914	17.00	55.00
1914-D	17.00	55.00
1914-S	235	620
1915	17.00	55.00
1915-D	17.00	55.00
1915-S	35.00	110
1916	17.00	55.00
1916-D	17.00	55.00

STANDING LIBERTY

The Standing Liberty design, by Hermon A. MacNeil, is considered one of the most beautiful in U.S. coinage history. The design originally depicted Liberty with her right breast exposed (Type 1). Because of public backlash, the design was modified so Liberty's breast was covered (Type 2).

The design was further modified in 1925. Previously, the date was in higher relief, which caused the numerals to wear off easily. In 1925, the date area was carved out, which allowed the numerals to be recessed into the design and better protect them from wear.

Liberty's head did not always strike up fully. As a result, examples with a "full head" command a premium.

Type 1

Size: *24.3 millimeters.* **Weight:** *6.25 grams.*
Composition: *90 percent silver (0.1809 troy ounces), 10 percent copper.*

	F	XF
1916	6,900	14,500
1917	65.00	120

	F	XF
1917-D	100	200
1917-S	110	220

In 1917 the obverse design was modified to cover Liberty's bare right breast.

	F	XF
1917	50.00	95.00
1917-D	90.00	160
1917-S	65.00	110
1918	30.00	45.00
1918-D	65.00	125
1918-S	35.00	50.00
1919	55.00	80.00
1919-D	200	565
1919-S	185	510
1920	25.00	50.00
1920-D	90.00	160
1920-S	30.00	55.00
1921	450	750
1923	35.00	55.00
1923-S	675	1,500
1924	25.00	45.00

	F	XF
1924-D	110	185
1924-S	45.00	100
1925	10.00	45.00
1926	8.75	30.00
1926-D	20.00	75.00
1926-S	11.00	110
1927	8.75	40.00
1927-D	30.00	140
1927-S	110	1,000
1928	8.75	30.00
1928-D	10.00	45.00
1929	8.75	30.00
1929-D	10.00	40.00
1929-S	9.25	35.00
1930	8.75	30.00
1930-S	8.75	35.00

WASHINGTON

The Washington quarter was intended to be a one-year issue commemorating the 200th anniversary of George Washington's birth, but it proved to be so popular that it permanently replaced the Standing Liberty quarter. John Flanagan's design is based on a 1785 bust of Washington by sculptor Jean Antoine Houdon.

Size: *24.3 millimeters.* **Weight:** *6.25 grams.*
Composition: *90 percent silver (0.1809 troy ounces), 10 percent copper.*

	VF	MS-60		VF	MS-60
1932	7.50	25.00	1938	9.00	90.00
1932-D	180	1,150	1938-S	10.00	110
1932-S	165	465	1939	8.25	15.00
1934	10.00	45.00	1939-D	9.75	40.00
1934-D	20.00	250	1939-S	12.00	100
1935	8.25	20.00	1940	8.25	17.50
1935-D	15.50	245	1940-D	12.50	130
1935-S	10.00	95.00	1940-S	8.00	30.00
1936	8.25	25.00	1941	7.00	9.50
1936-D	25.00	600	1941-D	8.00	35.00
1936-S	9.25	110	1941-S	8.25	30.00
1937	9.50	20.00	1942	7.00	9.25
1937-D	9.00	70.00	1942-D	8.00	18.00
1937-S	20.00	160	1942-S	8.00	70.00

	VF	MS-60
1943	7.00	9.00
1943-D	8.00	30.00
1943-S	8.25	25.00
1944	7.00	8.25
1944-D	8.00	20.00
1944-S	8.00	15.00
1945	7.00	8.25
1945-D	8.00	18.00
1945-S	7.75	8.50
1946	7.00	8.25
1946-D	8.00	9.75
1946-S	8.00	9.25
1947	8.00	11.50
1947-D	8.00	11.00
1947-S	8.00	9.50
1948	8.00	9.50
1948-D	8.00	13.00
1948-S	8.00	9.25
1949	8.00	35.00
1949-D	8.00	16.50
1950	7.00	10.00
1950-D	7.00	8.50
1950-S	8.00	15.00
1951	7.00	8.00
1951-D	7.00	9.00
1951-S	8.00	25.00
1952	7.00	11.50
1952-D	7.00	9.25

	VF	MS-60
1952-S	8.00	20.00
1953	7.00	10.00
1953-D	7.00	8.75
1953-S	7.00	9.00
1954	7.00	8.25
1954-D	7.00	8.25
1954-S	7.00	8.25
1955	7.00	8.25
1955-D	7.00	9.25
1956	7.00	8.25
1956-D	7.00	8.25
1957	7.00	8.25
1957-D	7.00	8.25
1958	7.00	8.25
1958-D	7.00	8.25
1959	7.00	8.25
1959-D	7.00	8.25
1960	7.00	8.25
1960-D	7.00	8.25
1961	7.00	8.25
1961-D	7.00	8.25
1962	7.00	8.25
1962-D	7.00	8.25
1963	7.00	8.25
1963-D	7.00	8.25
1964	7.00	8.25
1964-D	7.00	8.25

Clad composition

Size: 24.3 millimeters. **Weight:** 5.67 grams. **Composition:** Clad layers of 75 percent copper and 25 percent nickel bonded to a pure copper core.

	MS-65	PF-65
1965	12.00	—
1966	9.00	—
1967	12.00	—
1968	15.00	—
1968-D	8.00	—
1968-S	—	2.00
1969	14.00	—
1969-D	10.00	—
1969-S	—	2.25
1970	12.00	—
1970-D	9.50	—
1970-S	—	2.00

	MS-65	PF-65
1971	15.00	—
1971-D	6.50	—
1971-S	—	2.00
1972	7.50	—
1972-D	10.00	—
1972-S	—	2.00
1973	10.00	—
1973-D	12.50	—
1973-S	—	1.75
1974	8.00	—
1974-D	15.00	—
1974-S	—	2.00

Bicentennial reverse

A variety of coinage proposals for the nation's bicentennial emerged in the years leading up to the celebration. Among them were proposals for special commemorative coins (the U.S. Mint had not issued commemorative coins since 1954), redesigning all six circulating coins, issuing a 2-cent coin with a bicentennial design, and issuing a gold commemorative coin. The Mint and Treasury Department initially resisted any changes to circulating coin designs and the issuance of commemorative coins, but they eased their opposition as the various proposals were winnowed to a final bill that was signed into law Oct. 18, 1973, by President Richard M. Nixon. That bill called for quarters, half dollars, and dollar coins struck after July 4, 1975, to bear new reverse designs emblematic of the nation's bicentennial. The law also called for the coins to bear the dual date "1776-1976."

The law also authorized the Mint to strike the bicentennial coins in a 40 percent silver composition for inclusion in three-coin mint and proof sets for sale directly to collectors.

To select designs for the bicentennial coins, the Mint sponsored a contest open to all U.S. citizens. Jack L. Ahr of Arlington Heights, Ill., had his Revolutionary-era drummer boy design selected for the quarter.

	MS-65	PF-65
1976	8.00	—
1976-D	10.00	—
1976-S	—	3.25

Bicentennial reverse, silver composition

Weight: *5.75 grams.* **Composition:** *Clad layers of 80 percent silver and 20 percent copper bonded to a core of 20.9 percent silver and 79.1 percent copper (0.0739 total troy ounces of silver).*

	MS-65	PF-65
1976-S	6.00	4.50

Regular reverse resumed

Starting in 1992, Washington quarters in the traditional 90 percent silver composition were struck for inclusion in silver proof sets, which also included silver dimes and silver half dollars.

	MS-65	PF-65
1977	10.00	—
1977-D	8.00	—
1977-S	—	2.75
1978	9.00	—
1978-D	11.00	—
1978-S	—	2.75
1979	10.00	—

	MS-65	PF-65
1979-D	9.00	—
1979-S	—	2.50
1980-P	8.00	—
1980-D	8.50	—
1980-S	—	2.75
1981-P	8.00	—
1981-D	6.50	—

	MS-65	PF-65
1981-S	2.75	—
1982-P	28.00	—
1982-D	15.00	—
1982-S	—	2.75
1983-P	45.00	—
1983-D	30.00	—
1983-S	—	3.00
1984-P	16.00	—
1984-D	12.50	—
1984-S	—	3.00
1985-P	15.00	—
1985-D	10.00	—
1985-S	—	3.00
1986-P	12.00	—
1986-D	15.00	—
1986-S	—	3.00
1987-P	10.00	—
1987-D	10.00	—
1987-S	—	3.00
1988-P	16.00	—
1988-D	14.00	—
1988-S	—	3.00
1989-P	18.00	—
1989-D	7.50	—
1989-S	—	3.00
1990-P	17.00	—
1990-D	7.00	—
1990-S	—	4.50
1991-P	15.00	—
1991-D	12.00	—

	MS-65	PF-65
1991-S	—	3.00
1992-P	20.00	—
1992-D	27.50	—
1992-S	—	3.00
1992-S silver	—	5.00
1993-P	11.00	—
1993-D	14.00	—
1993-S	—	3.00
1993-S silver	—	6.50
1994-P	18.00	—
1994-D	8.00	—
1994-S	—	3.00
1994-S silver	—	8.50
1995-P	22.00	—
1995-D	20.00	—
1995-S	—	9.00
1995-S silver	—	10.00
1996-P	15.00	—
1996-D	14.00	—
1996-S	—	4.50
1996-S silver	—	9.50
1997-P	12.50	—
1997-D	16.00	—
1997-S	—	9.00
1997-S silver	—	10.00
1998-P	13.50	—
1998-D	13.50	—
1998-S	—	9.00
1998-S silver	—	8.50

50 STATE QUARTERS

President Bill Clinton signed the 50 States Commemorative Coin Act into law on Dec. 1, 1997. The bill provided that from 1999 through 2008, the quarter's reverse would be redesigned to honor each of the 50 states. Five new designs would be introduced each year, and each new design would honor a different state. The states would be honored in the order in which they ratified the Constitution or were admitted to the union.

The bill gave authority for final approval of the designs to the Treasury secretary. It required the secretary to consult with each state's governor or the governor's designee on the respective state's design. The law banned any "frivolous or inappropriate" design. It further prohibited the depiction of a head-and-shoulders bust of any person, living or dead, or any representation of a living person. The traditional bust of George Washington appears on the obverse of each coin.

The law also authorized the U.S. Mint to produce uncirculated and proof examples of the 50 State quarters for sale to collectors and to produce examples in 90 percent silver composition for sale to collectors.

Delaware	MS-65	PF-65
1999-P	4.00	—
1999-D	5.00	—
1999-S	—	3.50
1999-S silver	—	25.00

New Jersey	MS-65	PF-65
1999-P	5.00	—
1999-D	4.00	—
1999-S	—	3.50
1999-S silver	—	25.00

Pennsylvania	MS-65	PF-65
1999-P	5.00	—
1999-D	4.00	—
1999-S	—	3.50
1999-S silver	—	25.00

Georgia	MS-65	PF-65
1999-P	4.50	—
1999-D	4.50	—
1999-S	—	3.50
1999-S silver	—	25.00

Connecticut	MS-65	PF-65
1999-P	6.00	—
1999-D	5.00	—
1999-S	—	3.50
1999-S silver	—	25.00

South Carolina	MS-65	PF-65
2000-P	6.00	—
2000-D	9.00	—
2000-S	—	3.00
2000-S silver	—	9.00

Massachusetts	MS-65	PF-65
2000-P	5.50	—
2000-D	6.50	—
2000-S	—	3.00
2000-S silver	—	9.00

New Hampshire	MS-65	PF-65
2000-P	6.50	—
2000-D	7.50	—
2000-S	—	3.00
2000-S silver	—	9.00

Maryland	MS-65	PF-65
2000-P	6.00	—
2000-D	6.00	—
2000-S	—	3.00
2000-S silver	—	9.00

Virginia	MS-65	PF-65
2000-P	6.50	—
2000-D	6.50	—
2000-S	—	3.00
2000-S silver	—	9.00

New York	MS-65	PF-65
2001-P	5.50	—
2001-D	5.50	—
2001-S	—	4.00
2001-S silver	—	11.00

Vermont	MS-65	PF-65
2001-P	6.50	—
2001-D	6.50	—
2001-S	—	4.00
2001-S silver	—	11.00

North Carolina	MS-65	PF-65
2001-P	5.50	—
2001-D	6.50	—
2001-S	—	4.00
2001-S silver	—	11.00

Kentucky	MS-65	PF-65
2001-P	6.50	—
2001-D	7.00	—
2001-S	—	4.00
2001-S silver	—	11.00

Rhode Island	MS-65	PF-65
2001-P	5.50	—
2001-D	6.00	—
2001-S	—	4.00
2001-S silver	—	11.00

Tennessee	MS-65	PF-65
2002-P	6.50	—
2002-D	7.00	—
2002-S	—	2.50
2002-S silver	—	9.00

Ohio	MS-65	PF-65
2002-P	5.50	—
2002-D	5.50	—
2002-S	—	2.50
2002-S silver	—	9.00

Mississippi	MS-65	PF-65
2002-P	5.00	—
2002-D	5.00	—
2002-S	—	2.50
2002-S silver	—	9.00

Louisiana	MS-65	PF-65
2002-P	5.50	—
2002-D	6.00	—
2002-S	—	2.50
2002-S silver	—	9.00

Illinois	MS-65	PF-65
2003-P	5.00	—
2003-D	5.00	—
2003-S	—	2.50
2003-S silver	—	9.00

Indiana	MS-65	PF-65
2002-P	5.00	—
2002-D	5.00	—
2002-S	—	2.50
2002-S silver	—	9.00

Alabama	MS-65	PF-65
2003-P	5.00	—
2003-D	5.00	—
2003-S	—	2.50
2003-S silver	—	9.00

Maine	MS-65	PF-65
2003-P	5.00	—
2003-D	5.00	—
2003-S	—	2.50
2003-S silver	—	9.00

Michigan	MS-65	PF-65
2004-P	5.00	—
2004-D	5.00	—
2004-S	—	2.50
2004-S silver	—	9.00

Missouri	MS-65	PF-65
2003-P	5.00	—
2003-D	5.00	—
2003-S	—	2.50
2003-S silver	—	9.00

Florida	MS-65	PF-65
2004-P	5.00	—
2004-D	5.00	—
2004-S	—	2.50
2004-S silver	—	9.00

Arkansas	MS-65	PF-65
2003-P	5.00	—
2003-D	5.00	—
2003-S	—	2.50
2003-S silver	—	9.00

Texas	MS-65	PF-65
2004-P	5.00	—
2004-D	5.00	—
2004-S	—	2.50
2004-S silver	—	9.00

Iowa	MS-65	PF-65
2004-P	5.00	—
2004-D	5.00	—
2004-S	—	2.50
2004-S silver	—	9.00

Wisconsin	MS-65	PF-65
2004-P	5.00	—
2004-D	5.00	—
2004-S	—	2.50
2004-S silver	—	9.00

Minnesota	MS-65	PF-65
2005-P	5.00	—
2005-P satin finish	4.50	—
2005-D	5.00	—
2005-D satin finish	4.50	—
2005-S	—	2.50
2005-S silver	—	9.00

Oregon	MS-65	PF-65
2005-P	5.00	—
2005-P satin finish	4.50	—
2005-D	5.00	—
2005-D satin finish	4.50	—
2005-S	—	2.50
2005-S silver	—	9.00

Kansas	MS-65	PF-65
2005-P	5.00	—
2005-P satin finish	4.50	—
2005-D	5.00	—
2005-D satin finish	4.50	—
2005-S	—	2.50
2005-S silver	—	9.00

West Virginia	MS-65	PF-65
2005-P	5.00	—
2005-P satin finish	4.50	—
2005-D	5.00	—
2005-D satin finish	4.50	—
2005-S	—	2.50
2005-S silver	—	6.00

California	MS-65	PF-65
2005-P	5.00	—
2005-P satin finish	4.50	—
2005-D	5.00	—
2005-D satin finish	4.50	—
2005-S	—	2.50
2005-S silver	—	9.00

Nevada	MS-65	PF-65
2006-P	5.00	—
2006-P satin finish	4.50	—

2006-D	5.00	—
2006-D satin finish	4.50	—
2006-S	—	2.50
2006-S silver	—	9.00

Nebraska	MS-65	PF-65
2006-P	5.00	—
2006-P satin finish	4.50	—
2006-D	5.00	—
2006-D satin finish	4.50	—
2006-S	—	2.50
2006-S silver	—	9.00

Colorado	MS-65	PF-65
2006-P	5.00	—
2006-P satin finish	4.50	—
2006-D	5.00	—
2006-D satin finish	4.50	—
2006-S	—	2.50
2006-S silver	—	9.00

North Dakota	MS-65	PF-65
2006-P	5.00	—
2006-P satin finish	4.50	—
2006-D	5.00	—
2006-D satin finish	4.50	—
2006-S	—	2.50
2006-S silver	—	9.00

South Dakota	MS-65	PF-65
2006-P	5.00	—
2006-P satin finish	4.50	—
2006-D	5.00	—
2006-D satin finish	4.50	—
2006-S	—	2.50
2006-S silver	—	9.00

Montana	MS-65	PF-65
2007-P	8.00	—
2007-P satin finish	4.50	—

2007-D	5.00	—
2007-D satin finish	4.50	—
2007-S	—	2.50
2007-S silver	—	9.00

Washington	MS-65	PF-65
2007-P	5.00	—
2007-P satin finish	4.50	—
2007-D	5.00	—
2007-D satin finish	4.50	—
2007-S	—	2.50
2007-S silver	—	9.00

Idaho	MS-65	PF-65
2007-P	5.00	—
2007-P satin finish	4.50	—
2007-D	5.00	—
2007-D satin finish	4.50	—
2007-S	—	2.50
2007-S silver	—	9.00

Wyoming	MS-65	PF-65
2007-P	5.00	—
2007-P satin finish	4.50	—
2007-D	5.00	—
2007-D satin finish	4.50	—
2007-S	—	2.50
2007-S silver	—	9.00

Utah	MS-65	PF-65
2007-P	5.00	—
2007-P satin finish	4.50	—
2007-D	5.00	—
2007-D satin finish	4.50	—
2007-S	—	2.50
2007-S silver	—	9.00

Oklahoma	MS-65	PF-65
2008-P	5.00	—
2008-P satin finish	4.50	—

2008-D	5.00	—
2008-D satin finish	4.50	—
2008-S	—	2.50
2008-S silver	—	9.00

New Mexico	MS-65	PF-65
2008-P	5.00	—
2008-P satin finish	4.50	—
2008-D	5.00	—
2008-D satin finish	4.50	—
2008-S	—	2.50
2008-S silver	—	9.00

Arizona	MS-65	PF-65
2008-P	5.00	—
2008-P satin finish	4.50	—
2008-D	5.00	—
2008-D satin finish	4.50	—
2008-S	—	2.50
2008-S silver	—	9.00

Alaska	MS-65	PF-65
2008-P	5.00	—
2008-P satin finish	4.50	—
2008-D	5.00	—
2008-D satin finish	4.50	—
2008-S	—	2.50
2008-S silver	—	9.00

Hawaii	MS-65	PF-65
2008-P	5.00	—
2008-P satin finish	4.50	—
2008-D	5.00	—
2008-D satin finish	4.50	—
2008-S	—	2.50
2008-S silver	—	9.00

DISTRICT OF COLUMBIA AND U.S. TERRITORIES

Upon completion of the 50 State quarters program, the U.S. Mint issued circulating quarters honoring the District of Columbia and the five U.S. territories in 2009. The coins were released in two-month intervals beginning with the District of Columbia quarter in February 2009. It was followed, in order, by coins honoring Puerto Rico, Guam, American Samoa, U.S. Virgin Islands, and the Northern Mariana Islands.

The traditional bust of George Washington appears on the obverse of each coin. As with the State quarters, the authorizing legislation provided for uncirculated, proof, and 90 percent-silver versions of the coins for sale to collectors.

District of Columbia	MS-65	PF-65
2009-P	8.00	—
2009-D	8.00	—
2009-S	—	4.00
2009-S silver	—	6.50

American Samoa	MS-65	PF-65
2009-P	8.00	—
2009-D	8.00	—
2009-S	—	4.00
2009-S silver	—	6.50

Puerto Rico	MS-65	PF-65
2009-P	8.00	—
2009-D	8.00	—
2009-S	—	4.00
2009-S silver	—	6.50

U.S. Virgin Islands	MS-65	PF-65
2009-P	8.00	—
2009-D	8.00	—
2009-S	—	4.00
2009-S silver	—	6.50

Guam	MS-65	PF-65
2009-P	8.00	—
2009-D	8.00	—
2009-S	—	4.00
2009-S silver	—	6.50

Northern Mariana Islands	MS-65	PF-65
2009-P	8.00	—
2009-D	8.00	—
2009-S	—	4.00
2009-S silver	—	6.50

AMERICA THE BEAUTIFUL QUARTERS

The America the Beautiful quarters program (a U.S. Mint trademark) will continue the issuance of circulating quarters with commemorative reverse designs. Five different reverse designs honoring national parks and national sites will be issued in each year from 2010 through 2020. The final issue in the 56-coin series is scheduled for release in 2021. Every state, U.S. territory, and the District of Columbia will be represented in the series. The traditional bust of George Washington will appear on the obverse of each coin.

Like the state and territories quarters, the authorizing legislation again provides for the issuance of uncirculated, proof, and 90 percent silver versions of the coins for sale to collectors.

Hot Springs	MS-65	PF-65
2010-P	8.00	—
2010-D	8.00	—
2010-S	—	4.00
2010-S silver	—	6.50

Yosemite	MS-65	PF-65
2010-P	8.00	—
2010-D	8.00	—
2010-S	—	4.00
2010-S silver	—	6.50

Yellowstone	MS-65	PF-65
2010-P	8.00	—
2010-D	8.00	—
2010-S	—	4.00
2010-S silver	—	6.50

Grand Canyon	MS-65	PF-65
2010-P	8.00	—
2010-D	8.00	—
2010-S	—	4.00
2010-S silver	—	6.50

Mount Hood	MS-65	PF-65
2010-P	8.00	—
2010-D	8.00	—
2010-S	—	4.00
2010-S silver	—	6.50

Olympic	MS-65	PF-65
2011-P	8.00	—
2011-D	8.00	—
2011-S	—	4.00
2011-S silver	—	6.50

Gettysburg	MS-65	PF-65
2011-P	8.00	—
2011-D	8.00	—
2011-S	—	4.00
2011-S silver	—	6.50

Vicksburg	MS-65	PF-65
2011-P	8.00	—
2011-D	8.00	—
2011-S	—	4.00
2011-S silver	—	6.50

Glacier	MS-65	PF-65
2011-P	8.00	—
2011-D	8.00	—
2011-S	—	4.00
2011-S silver	—	6.50

Chickasaw	MS-65	PF-65
2011-P	8.00	—
2011-D	8.00	—
2011-S	—	4.00
2011-S silver	—	6.50

El Yunque	MS-65	PF-65
2012-P	—	—
2012-D	—	—
2012-S	—	—
2012-S silver	—	—

Hawai'i Volcanoes	MS-65	PF-65
2012-P	—	—
2012-D	—	—
2012-S	—	—
2012-S silver	—	—

Chaco Culture	MS-65	PF-65
2012-P	—	—
2012-D	—	—
2012-S	—	—
2012-S silver	—	—

Denali	MS-65	PF-65
2012-P	—	—
2012-D	—	—
2012-S	—	—
2012-S silver	—	—

Acadia	MS-65	PF-65
2012-P	—	—
2012-D	—	—
2012-S	—	—
2012-S silver	—	—

Half dollars

FLOWING HAIR

The half dollar was among the denominations originally authorized in 1792, with production beginning in 1794. The Flowing Hair design is similar to the one used on the first issues of smaller denominations.

There are many die varieties among early half dollars. The scarcer ones command a premium over the more common ones. Also, early half dollars were struck on planchets with crude edges. They often are found with "adjustment marks" that resulted from filing off the excess metal before striking.

Size: *32.5 millimeters.* **Weight:** *13.48 grams.* **Composition:** *89.24 percent silver (0.3869 troy ounces), 10.76 percent copper.*

	VG	VF
1794	5,750	19,500
1795	1,470	5,200

DRAPED BUST

A more attractive portrait of Liberty was introduced on the 1796 half dollar. Also, the denomination, indicated as the fraction "1/2," was added to the reverse below the eagle for 1796 and 1797.

After a three-year lapse, half dollar production resumed in 1801 with a new, heraldic-style eagle appearing on the reverse, but the denomination was removed.

Small eagle

Size: *32.5 millimeters.* **Weight:** *13.48 grams.* **Composition:** *89.24 percent silver (0.3869 troy ounces), 10.76 percent copper.*

	VG	VF
1796 15 stars	46,000	73,500
1796 16 stars	50,000	79,500
1797	46,300	74,300

	VG	VF		VG	VF
1801	1,250	4,250	1805	235	685
1802	1,350	4,500	1806	235	665
1803 small 3	325	825	1807	235	665
1803 large 3	235	715			

LIBERTY CAP

A new design for the half dollar in 1807 saw Liberty turned around – from facing the viewer's right to facing the viewer's left – and a cap added to her head. The reverse was also redesigned, and the denomination, indicated as "50 C.," also reappeared on the coin. The style used to indicate the denomination changed twice during the coin's production run, as noted in the listings that follow.

Many 1807-1839 half dollars were stored in bank vaults in the early 1900s as cash backing for the banks' privately issued paper money. As a result, many well-preserved examples are available today. Some, however, are weakly struck, particularly in the motto above the eagle on the reverse.

Size: *32.5 millimeters.* **Weight:** *13.48 grams.* **Composition:** *89.24 percent silver (0.3869 troy ounces), 10.76 percent.*

	VG	VF
1807	170	700
1808	85.00	145
1809	80.00	140
1810	80.00	135
1811	80.00	125
1812	80.00	110
1813	80.00	110
1814	80.00	120
1815	1,550	3,650
1817	85.00	115
1818	80.00	115
1819	80.00	115
1820	90.00	150
1821	75.00	100
1822	75.00	100

	VG	VF
1823	75.00	100
1824	75.00	100
1825	75.00	100
1826	75.00	100
1827	75.00	100
1828	75.00	100
1829	70.00	85.00
1830	80.00	100
1831	70.00	85.00
1832	75.00	90.00
1833	70.00	85.00
1834	75.00	90.00
1835	70.00	85.00
1836	70.00	85.00

Reeded edge, "50 Cents" on reverse

Size: *30 millimeters.* **Weight:** *13.36 grams.* **Composition:** *90 percent silver (0.3867 troy ounces), 10 percent copper.*

	VG	VF
1836	1,075	2,000
1837	75.00	115

"Half Dol." on reverse

	VG	VF
1838	70.00	120
1838-O		*proof* 250,000
1839	75.00	130
1839-O	325	650

SEATED LIBERTY

Christian Gobrecht's Seated Liberty design first appeared on the dollar and was later adapted for the lower denominations. The Seated Liberty half dollar underwent a number of modifications in design and specifications during its long run, as noted in the listings that follow. In some cases, a design tweak indicated a change in specifications.

Size: *30.6 millimeters.* **Weight:** *13.36 grams.* **Composition:** *90 percent silver (0.3867 troy ounces), 10 percent copper.* **Notes:** *Some 1839 strikes have drapery extending from Liberty's left elbow.*

	VG	VF		VG	VF
1839 no drapery	80.00	335	1846	45.00	65.00
1839 with drapery	40.00	85.00	1846-O	40.00	65.00
1840	40.00	85.00	1847	45.00	65.00
1840-O	50.00	90.00	1847-O	40.00	65.00
1841	65.00	150	1848	65.00	185
1841-O	45.00	80.00	1848-O	40.00	70.00
1842	40.00	65.00	1849	45.00	65.00
1842-O	45.00	90.00	1849-O	40.00	70.00
1843	40.00	65.00	1850	325	550
1843-O	40.00	65.00	1850-O	40.00	80.00
1844	40.00	65.00	1851	450	850
1844-O	40.00	70.00	1851-O	55.00	120
1845	45.00	125	1852	500	925
1845-O no drapery	45.00	115	1852-O	125	350
1845-O with drapery	40.00	70.00	1853-O *rare*		

Arrows at date, reverse rays

Size: *30.6 millimeters.* **Weight:** *12.44 grams.*
Composition: *90 percent silver (0.36 troy ounces), 10 percent copper.*

	VG	VF
1853	35.00	90.00
1853-O	40.00	115

Reverse rays removed

	VG	VF
1854	40.00	60.00
1854-O	40.00	60.00
1855	40.00	65.00

	VG	VF
1855-O	40.00	60.00
1855-S	475	1,500

Arrows at date removed

	VG	VF
1856	40.00	70.00
1856-O	40.00	60.00
1856-S	120	260
1857	40.00	60.00
1857-O	40.00	85.00
1857-S	120	285
1858	40.00	70.00
1858-O	40.00	70.00
1858-S	50.00	110
1859	40.00	70.00
1859-O	40.00	70.00
1859-S	45.00	100
1860	40.00	100
1860-O	40.00	70.00
1860-S	45.00	80.00

	VG	VF
1861	40.00	70.00
1861-O	45.00	80.00
1861-S	45.00	85.00
1862	50.00	120
1862-S	40.00	75.00
1863	50.00	85.00
1863-S	45.00	70.00
1864	50.00	120
1864-S	45.00	70.00
1865	50.00	90.00
1865-S	45.00	70.00
1866 *proof, one known*		
1866-S	575	1,250

Motto above eagle

	VG	VF
1866	45.00	80.00
1866-S	45.00	70.00
1867	50.00	110
1867-S	40.00	70.00
1868	55.00	185
1868-S	40.00	70.00
1869	45.00	70.00
1869-S	45.00	70.00
1870	45.00	80.00
1870-CC	1,500	3,900

	VG	VF
1870-S	45.00	85.00
1871	40.00	75.00
1871-CC	325	1,200
1871-S	40.00	70.00
1872	40.00	75.00
1872-CC	125	400
1872-S	45.00	135
1873 closed 3	45.00	100
1873 open 3	3,400	5,500
1873-CC	320	950

Arrows at date

Size: *30.6 millimeters.* **Weight:** *12.5 grams.*
Composition: *90 percent silver (0.3618 troy ounces), 10 percent copper.*

	VG	VF
1873	50.00	90.00
1873-CC	275	850
1873-S	80.00	245

	VG	VF
1874	40.00	85.00
1874-CC	575	1,750
1874-S	65.00	185

Arrows at date removed

	VG	VF
1875	40.00	55.00
1875-CC	55.00	125
1875-S	40.00	65.00
1876	40.00	55.00
1876-CC	60.00	100
1876-S	40.00	55.00
1877	40.00	55.00
1877-CC	55.00	115
1877-S	40.00	55.00
1878	45.00	80.00
1878-CC	525	1,500
1878-S	37,500	47,500
1879	310	400

	VG	VF
1880	280	355
1881	300	385
1882	365	450
1883	340	435
1884	375	500
1885	425	550
1886	500	700
1887	525	775
1888	300	400
1889	315	400
1890	310	415
1891	75.00	120

BARBER

The dime, quarter, and half dollar were all revised in 1892 to depict a right-facing portrait of Liberty designed by U.S. Mint Chief Engraver Charles Barber, for whom they have been popularly named.

Barber half dollars are common, and well-worn examples are worth bullion value only. But the series is popular among collectors, resulting in solid demand and, thus, strong values in middle grades.

Size: *30.6 millimeters.* **Weight:** *12.5 grams.*
Composition: *90 percent silver (0.3618 troy ounces). 10 percent copper.*

	VG	VF		VG	VF
1892	40.00	120	1896-S	145	350
1892-O	420	575	1897	20.00	100
1892-S	330	530	1897-O	230	835
1893	35.00	135	1897-S	225	535
1893-O	65.00	220	1898	20.00	95.00
1893-S	225	500	1898-O	75.00	355
1894	50.00	200	1898-S	55.00	175
1894-O	35.00	170	1899	20.00	100
1894-S	30.00	125	1899-O	40.00	170
1895	25.00	150	1899-S	40.00	135
1895-O	45.00	195	1900	20.00	90.00
1895-S	55.00	235	1900-O	25.00	165
1896	30.00	160	1900-S	20.00	100
1896-O	55.00	290	1901	20.00	95.00

	VG	VF
1901-O	25.00	200
1901-S	55.00	355
1902	15.00	85.00
1902-O	17.00	100
1902-S	20.00	150
1903	20.00	100
1903-O	17.00	115
1903-S	20.00	125
1904	15.00	85.00
1904-O	30.00	220
1904-S	75.00	555
1905	35.00	180
1905-O	45.00	235
1905-S	20.00	125
1906	15.00	85.00
1906-D	15.00	90.00
1906-O	15.00	100
1906-S	17.00	110
1907	15.00	85.00
1907-D	15.00	75.00
1907-O	15.00	90.00
1907-S	20.00	165
1908	15.00	80.00

	VG	VF
1908-D	15.00	80.00
1908-O	15.00	90.00
1908-S	25.00	160
1909	20.00	85.00
1909-O	25.00	140
1909-S	15.00	100
1910	30.00	170
1910-S	20.00	100
1911	15.00	85.00
1911-D	20.00	90.00
1911-S	20.00	100
1912	15.00	85.00
1912-D	15.00	80.00
1912-S	20.00	100
1913	90.00	420
1913-D	20.00	100
1913-S	25.00	110
1914	175	550
1914-S	20.00	100
1915	170	380
1915-D	15.00	75.00
1915-S	20.00	95.00

WALKING LIBERTY

Adolph Weinman's Walking Liberty half dollar design is an all-time favorite among collectors. (Weinman also designed the Mercury dime.) The design was reprised in 1986 for the new silver American Eagle bullion coins.

Mintmarks on the Walking Liberty half dollar originally appeared on the obverse, but they were moved to the reverse in 1917. Watch for genuine 1916 and 1938 examples with mintmarks fraudulently added to emulate the more rare 1916-S and 1938-D.

Liberty's head did not always strike up fully. High-grade examples with Liberty's head fully struck command a premium.

Size: *30.6 millimeters.* **Weight:** *12.5 grams.* **Composition:** *90 percent silver (0.3618 troy ounces), 10 percent copper.* **Notes:** *The mintmark appears on the obverse below the word "Trust" on all 1916 strikes and some 1917 strikes. It was then moved to the reverse at approximately the 8 o'clock position.*

	F	XF
1916	95.00	240
1916-D	80.00	220
1916-S	280	600
1917 reverse mintmark	15.00	40.00
1917-D obverse mintmark	80.00	235
1917-S obverse mintmark	135	700
1917-D reverse mintmark	45.00	275

	F	XF
1917-S reverse mintmark	17.00	65.00
1918	15.00	150
1918-D	35.00	225
1918-S	16.00	60.00
1919	80.00	535
1919-D	95.00	765
1919-S	70.00	825
1920	15.00	75.00
1920-D	65.00	460
1920-S	20.00	235

	F	XF		F	XF
1921	350	1,575	1939-D	15.00	18.00
1921-D	550	2,200	1939-S	15.00	25.00
1921-S	210	4,850	1940	15.00	17.00
1923-S	30.00	300	1940-S	15.00	20.00
1927-S	17.00	165	1941	15.00	16.00
1928-S	20.00	200	1941-D	15.00	16.00
1929-D	18.00	100	1941-S	15.00	20.00
1929-S	15.00	115	1942	15.00	16.00
1933-S	18.00	60.00	1942-D	15.00	16.00
1934	15.00	17.00	1942-S	15.00	16.00
1934-D	20.00	35.00	1943	15.00	16.00
1934-S	15.00	30.00	1943-D	15.00	16.00
1935	15.00	18.00	1943-S	15.00	16.00
1935-D	15.00	35.00	1944	15.00	16.00
1935-S	15.00	30.00	1944-D	15.00	16.00
1936	15.00	18.00	1944-S	15.00	16.00
1936-D	15.00	20.00	1945	15.00	16.00
1936-S	15.00	20.00	1945-D	15.00	16.00
1937	15.00	18.00	1945-S	15.00	16.00
1937-D	17.00	35.00	1946	15.00	16.00
1937-S	15.00	25.00	1946-D	15.00	25.00
1938	15.00	20.00	1946-S	15.00	17.00
1938-D	100	185	1947	15.00	16.00
1939	15.00	18.00	1947-D	15.00	16.00

U.S. Mint Director Nellie Tayloe Ross was apparently the driving force behind the change from the Walking Liberty half dollar to the Franklin half dollar in 1948. Ross had wanted to introduce a coin honoring Franklin for some time. According to some historical accounts, she also considered the cent because of Franklin's saying "A penny saved is twopence clear," which evolved into "A penny saved is a penny earned."

U.S. Mint Chief Engraver John Sinnock's bust of Franklin on the obverse is a composite based on several portraits. The Liberty Bell depiction on the reverse is based on the 1926 U.S. Sesquicentennial commemorative half dollar, also designed by Sinnock. A small eagle was added to the right of the bell because coinage laws require that all denominations larger than a dime include a depiction of an eagle.

Mint state examples with fully struck lines across the bell command a premium.

Size: *30.6 millimeters.* **Weight:** *12.5 grams.*
Composition: *90 percent silver (0.3618 troy ounces), 10 percent copper.*

	XF	MS-60		XF	MS-60
1948	15.00	16.00	1952-D	14.00	17.00
1948-D	14.50	16.00	1952-S	15.00	50.00
1949	15.00	40.00	1953	15.00	25.00
1949-D	16.50	45.00	1953-D	13.50	15.00
1949-S	16.50	60.00	1953-S	15.00	25.00
1950	14.00	25.00	1954	13.50	15.00
1950-D	15.00	20.00	1954-D	13.50	15.00
1951	13.50	17.00	1954-S	14.00	15.00
1951-D	18.00	25.00	1955	18.00	20.00
1951-S	14.50	25.00	1956	14.00	15.00
1952	14.00	17.00	1957	14.00	15.00

	XF	MS-60
1957-D	14.00	15.00
1958	14.00	15.00
1958-D	14.00	15.00
1959	14.00	15.00
1959-D	14.00	15.00
1960	14.00	15.00
1960-D	14.00	15.00

	XF	MS-60
1961	14.00	15.00
1961-D	14.00	15.00
1962	14.00	15.00
1962-D	14.00	15.00
1963	14.00	15.00
1963-D	14.00	15.00

KENNEDY

It was only days after John F. Kennedy's assassination on Nov. 22, 1963, when proposals to honor the slain president on a coin emerged. The quarter, half dollar, and dollar were all considered before the half dollar was chosen. Congress approved the design change quickly so production could begin with the new year's coinage in January 1964.

Work on the Kennedy half dollar began at the U.S. Mint even before the authorizing legislation was signed into law. To accommodate the tight turnaround time from concept to production, it was decided to adapt artwork already in-house. Kennedy's portrait on the obverse and the presidential seal on the reverse were both based on his official presidential medal. U.S. Mint Chief Engraver Gilroy Roberts had designed the medal's obverse, so he worked on adapting it for the half dollar. His assistant engraver, Frank Gasparro, who later succeeded Roberts as chief engraver, had designed the medal's reverse, so he worked on adapting it for the half dollar.

Kennedy half dollars have been struck in several different compositions, as noted in the listings that follow.

Coins dated 1970-D, 1987-P, and 1987-D were not issued for circulation but are widely available from broken-up Mint uncirculated sets.

Size: *30.6 millimeters.* **Weight:** *12.5 grams.*
Composition: *90 percent silver (0.3618 troy ounces), 10 percent copper.*

	MS-65	PF-65
1964	20.00	14.50

	MS-65	PF-65
1964-D	24.00	—

40 percent silver composition

Weight: *11.5 grams.* **Composition:** *Clad layers of 80 percent silver and 20 percent copper bonded to a core of 20.9 percent silver and 79.1 percent copper (0.148 total troy ounces of silver).*

	MS-65	PF-65
1965	18.00	—
1966	14.00	—
1967	22.00	—
1968-D	18.00	—
1968-S	—	7.00

	MS-65	PF-65
1969-D	20.00	—
1969-S	—	7.00
1970-D	50.00	—
1970-S	—	20.00

Clad composition

Weight: *11.34 grams.* **Composition:** *Clad layers of 75 percent copper and 25 percent nickel bonded to a pure copper core.*

	MS-65	PF-65
1971	15.00	—
1971-D	15.00	—
1971-S	—	8.00
1972	20.00	—
1972-D	14.00	—
1972-S	—	7.00

	MS-65	PF-65
1973	14.00	—
1973-D	12.00	—
1973-S	—	7.00
1974	18.00	—
1974-D	20.00	—
1974-S	—	6.00

Bicentennial reverse

A variety of coinage proposals for the nation's bicentennial emerged in the years leading up to the celebration. Among them were proposals for special commemorative coins (the U.S. Mint had not issued commemorative coins since 1954), redesigning all six circulating coins, issuing a 2-cent coin with a bicentennial design, and issuing a gold commemorative coin. The Mint and Treasury Department initially resisted any changes to circulating coin designs and the issuance of commemorative coins, but they eased their opposition as the various proposals were winnowed to a final bill that was signed into law Oct. 18, 1973, by President Richard M. Nixon. That bill called for quarters, half dollars, and dollar coins struck after July 4, 1975, to bear new reverse designs emblematic of the nation's Bicentennial. The law also called for the coins to bear the dual date "1776-1976."

The law also authorized the Mint to strike the bicentennial coins in a 40 percent silver composition for inclusion in three-coin mint and proof sets for sale directly to collectors.

To select designs for the bicentennial coins, the Mint sponsored a contest open to all U.S. citizens. Seth G. Huntington of Minneapolis had his Independence Hall design selected for the half dollar.

	MS-65	PF-65
1976	22.00	—
1976-D	9.00	—
1976-S	—	5.00

Weight: *11.5 grams.* **Composition:** *Clad layers of 80 percent silver and 20 percent copper bonded to a core of 20.9 percent silver and 79.1 percent copper (0.148 troy ounces of silver).*

	MS-65	PF-65
1976-S	12.00	6.00

Regular reverse resumed

Starting in 1992, Kennedy half dollars in the traditional 90 percent silver composition were struck for inclusion in silver proof sets, which also included silver dimes and silver quarters.

	MS-65	PF-65			MS-65	PF-65
1977	18.00	—		1983-P	20.00	—
1977-D	20.00	—		1983-D	10.00	—
1977-S	—	4.50		1983-S	—	6.50
1978	12.00	—		1984-P	13.00	—
1978-D	10.00	—		1984-D	18.00	—
1978-S	—	6.00		1984-S	—	7.00
1979	11.00	—		1985-P	10.00	—
1979-D	9.00	—		1985-D	12.00	—
1979-S	—	6.00		1985-S	—	6.00
1980-P	9.00	—		1986-P	25.00	—
1980-D	6.50	—		1986-D	17.00	—
1980-S	—	6.00		1986-S	—	8.00
1981-P	8.00	—		1987-P	14.00	—
1981-D	8.50	—		1987-D	10.00	—
1981-S	—	5.00		1987-S	—	6.50
1982-P	10.00	—		1988-P	16.00	—
1982-D	9.00	—		1988-D	12.00	—
1982-S	—	6.50		1988-S	—	6.00

	MS-65	PF-65
1989-P	18.00	—
1989-D	14.00	—
1989-S	—	8.00
1990-P	18.00	—
1990-D	15.00	—
1990-S	—	7.00
1991-P	15.00	—
1991-D	16.00	—
1991-S	—	13.00
1992-P	12.00	—
1992-D	8.00	—
1992-S	—	8.00
1992-S silver	—	14.50
1993-P	15.00	—
1993-D	14.00	—
1993-S	—	14.00
1993-S silver	—	32.00
1994-P	8.00	—
1994-D	8.00	—
1994-S	—	11.00
1994-S silver	—	35.00
1995-P	9.00	—
1995-D	8.00	—
1995-S	—	35.00
1995-S silver	—	90.00
1996-P	10.00	—
1996-D	8.00	—
1996-S	—	16.00
1996-S silver	—	40.00

	MS-65	PF-65
1997-P	14.00	—
1997-D	10.00	—
1997-S	—	35.00
1997-S silver	—	75.00
1998-P	12.50	—
1998-D	12.50	—
1998-S	—	20.00
1998-S silver	—	25.00
1999-P	9.00	—
1999-D	9.00	—
1999-S	—	18.00
1999-S silver	—	40.00
2000-P	9.00	—
2000-D	7.00	—
2000-S	—	8.00
2000-S silver	—	14.50
2001-P	9.00	—
2001-D	9.00	—
2001-S	—	8.00
2001-S silver	—	20.00
2002-P	10.00	—
2002-D	10.00	—
2002-S	—	8.00
2002-S silver	—	14.50
2003-P	14.00	—
2003-D	14.00	—
2003-S	—	6.00
2003-S silver	—	14.50
2004-P	7.00	—

	MS-65	PF-65
2004-D	7.00	—
2004-S	—	13.00
2004-S silver	—	14.50
2005-P	9.00	—
2005-P satin finish	8.00	—
2005-D	9.00	—
2005-D satin finish	10.00	—
2005-S	—	7.00
2005-S silver	—	14.50
2006-P	12.00	—
2006-P satin finish	12.00	—
2006-D	20.00	—
2006-D satin finish	14.00	—
2006-S	—	10.00
2006-S silver	—	14.50
2007-P	7.00	—
2007-P satin finish	8.00	—
2007-D	7.00	—
2007-D satin finish	8.00	—
2007-S	—	10.00
2007-S silver	—	14.50
2008-P	7.00	—
2008-P satin finish	8.50	—
2008-D	7.00	—

	MS-65	PF-65
2008-D satin finish	8.50	—
2008-S	—	12.00
2008-S silver	—	14.50
2009-P	7.00	—
2009-P satin finish	8.50	—
2009-D	7.00	—
2009-D satin finish	8.50	—
2009-S	—	6.00
2009-S silver	—	20.00
2010-P	7.00	—
2010-P satin finish	8.50	—
2010-D	7.00	—
2010-D satin finish	8.50	—
2010-S	—	6.00
2010-S silver	—	20.00
2011-P	7.00	—
2011-D	7.00	—
2011-S,	—	6.00
2011-S silver	—	20.00

Silver dollars

FLOWING HAIR

The first U.S. silver dollar was intended to replace the Spanish colonial milled dollar, which popularly circulated in the country during Colonial days. It was one of the first silver denominations the U.S. Mint released, and it used the flowing-hair design of other early U.S. coins.

The denomination is designated on the edge as "Hundred Cents, One Dollar or Unit."

Early silver dollars were struck on planchets with crude edges. They often are found with "adjustment marks" that resulted from filing off the excess metal before striking. Although considered part of the manufacturing process, the marks still reduce a coin's value.

Watch for genuine 1795 Flowing Hair silver dollars that have been fraudulently re-engraved to appear to be the more scarce 1794.

Size: *39-40 millimeters.* **Weight:** *26.96 grams.*
Composition: *89.24 percent silver (0.7737 troy ounces), 10.76 percent copper.*

	VG	VF
1794	90,000	170,000
1795	2,200	7,500

DRAPED BUST

A more attractive Draped Bust design was introduced on the silver dollar in 1795. In 1798, the rather scrawny-looking eagle on the reverse was replaced by a more dignified heraldic eagle. The denomination continued to appear on the edge as "Hundred Cents, One Dollar or Unit."

Production of silver dollars for circulation was suspended after 1804 because of a lack of bullion and skilled labor to produce the coins. Also, the coins contained more silver than the Spanish dollar, but the Spanish dollar could still be exchanged at par for the silver dollar. As a result, many U.S. silver dollars were exported, melted, and replaced with Spanish dollars.

It is believed that the silver dollars struck for circulation in 1804 were dated 1803 to use up the inventory of dies leftover from 1803. Sometime during 1834-1835, a number of Draped Bust dollars dated 1804 were struck for inclusion in presentation proof sets to U.S. and foreign dignitaries. A few more 1804 dollars were struck again in 1859 for collectors.

Fifteen authentic 1804 silver dollars are known to exist today, and they are among numismatics' great rarities.

Small eagle

Size: *39-40 millimeters.* **Weight:** *26.96 grams.* **Composition:** *89.24 percent silver (0.7737 troy ounces), 10.76 percent copper.*

	VG	VF
1795	2,100	6,000
1796	2,100	6,500
1797	2,300	6,500
1798 13 stars	2,150	6,300
1798 15 stars	2,750	7,450

Heraldic eagle

	VG	VF
1798	1,185	2,735
1799	1,150	2,700
1800	1,200	3,000
1801	1,300	3,200

	VG	VF
1802	1,275	3,000
1803	1,300	3,000
1804 *15 known*		

SEATED LIBERTY

Christian Gobrecht's Seated Liberty design first appeared on a silver dollar in 1836. Gobrecht dollars, as they are commonly called, were also struck in 1838 and 1839, but they saw limited production, and many of the varieties produced during those years are considered patterns. Some restrikes produced in later years also exist.

After a 36-year lapse, production of silver dollars for circulation began again in 1840 using a version of Gobrecht's original 1836 design. The lettered edge used on early silver dollars was replaced by a reeded edge.

Size: *38.1 millimeters.* **Weight:** *26.73 grams.*
Composition: *90 percent silver (0.7736 troy ounces), 10 percent copper.*

	F	XF
1840	340	680
1841	315	610
1842	315	630
1843	315	465
1844	360	785
1845	385	900
1846	345	650
1846-O	370	775
1847	315	465
1848	515	1,250
1849	350	600
1850	380	1,750
1850-O	515	1,550
1851	5,750	18,000
1852	5,200	15,000
1853	550	1,100

	F	XF
1854	2,000	4,500
1855	1,500	3,750
1856	650	1,650
1857	675	1,500
1858 *proof, restrike*	4,000	7,250
1859	400	655
1989-O	315	465
1859-S	515	1,550
1860	380	660
1860-O	315	465
1861	900	1,750
1862	850	1,450
1863	575	985
1864	500	920
1865	420	1,050
1866 *2 known*		

Motto above eagle

	F	XF
1866	440	800
1867	400	670
1868	400	650
1869	370	640
1870	350	600

	F	XF
1870-CC	825	3,650
1870-S *12-15 known*		
1871	330	545
1871-CC	4,750	14,500

	F	XF
1872	330	500
1872-CC	2,850	4,850
1872-S	550	2,000

	F	XF
1873	340	510
1873-CC	11,500	31,500

TRADE DOLLAR

Trade dollars were struck to facilitate trade with Southeast Asia. They were largely intended to compete against the Mexican peso, which had slightly more silver than a standard dollar, and trade coins of other countries.

The legal-tender status of Trade dollars initially was limited in the United States, but in 1876, when the price of silver dropped, they ceased to be legal tender altogether until their status was restored in 1965. Eighteen million were redeemed by the government in 1887. Only proof examples were struck from 1879 to 1885.

It was common for Asian merchants to impress a character into Trade dollars and other silver coins to confirm that they accepted them as good quality. These "chop marks" are commonly found on Trade dollars; some have several marks. They reduce a coin's value because they are considered mutilation, but some numismatists have researched the marks. Chop-marked Trade dollars are not as valuable as unmarked examples, but they are still collectible.

Size: *38.1 millimeters.* **Weight:** *27.22 grams.* **Composition:** *90 percent silver (0.7878 troy ounces), 10 percent copper.* **Notes:** *Trade dollars were struck to facilitate trade with Southeast Asia.*

	F	XF
1873	165	250
1873-CC	330	700
1873-S	155	265
1874	150	250
1874-CC	310	600
1874-S	160	235
1875	375	590
1875-CC	285	510
1875-S	150	225
1876	160	235
1876-CC	300	525
1875-S	150	225
1877	160	235
1877-CC	320	700
1877-S	150	225

	F	XF
1878		*proof* 1,300
1878-CC	710	2,400
1878-S	150	225
1879		*proof* 1,275
1880		*proof* 1,250
1881		*proof* 1,300
1882		*proof* 1,275
1883		*proof* 1,300
1884		*proof* 100,000
1885 *proof, rare*		

MORGAN

The Morgan dollar – named for its designer, George T. Morgan – was introduced in response to pressure from silver-mining interests to remove excess silver from the market. For decades, silver dollars were scarce in circulation. With the boom in silver mining, the price of the metal dropped as supplies increased.

The new design marked the reintroduction of circulating silver dollars after a five-year absence. Because they were inconvenient to carry and use, however, perhaps hundreds of thousands of these dollars sat for decades in bags held as private, bank, and government reserves. The U.S. Treasury was stuck with such an excess that thousands remained on hand for almost a century, prompting the famous General Services Administration auction of silver dollars in the 1970s. They were sold in specially made cases, and Morgan dollars in the GSA cases often command a slight premium.

Morgan dollars have long been popular among collectors because of their appealing design, their large size, and the lore of silver dollars. But because large quantities of the coin survived, they remain affordable in nice circulated grades.

Collecting uncirculated Morgan dollars, however, requires a higher level of expertise and a bigger pocketbook. Because of their popularity and subsequent demand, a one-point difference in higher uncirculated grades can be the difference between hundreds or even thousands of dollars in value. That demand is further fueled by those who promote Morgan dollars as investments.

Strike quality among Morgan dollars can vary from mint to mint. San Francisco Mint examples are usually fully struck, Philadelphia strikes are of medium quality, and New Orleans dollars are usually the most weakly struck. The differences are most obvious on the eagle's breast.

Size: *38.1 millimeters.* **Weight:** *26.73 grams.* **Composition:** *90 percent silver (0.7736 troy ounces), 10 percent copper.* **Notes:** *The 1878 "8 tail feathers" and "7 tail feathers" varieties are distinguished by the number of feathers in the eagle's tail. On the "reverse of 1878" varieties, the top of the top feather in the arrows held by the eagle is straight across and the eagle's breast is concave. On the "reverse of 1878 varieties," the top of the top feather in the arrows held by the eagle is slanted and the eagle's breast is convex.*

	VF	MS-60
1878 8 tail feathers	40.00	135
1878 7-over-8 tail feathers	35.00	140
1878 7 tail feathers, reverse of 1878	35.00	65.00
1878 7 tail feathers, reverse of 1879	35.00	80.00
1878-CC	100	225
1878-S	35.00	65.00

	VF	MS-60
1879	35.00	45.00
1879-CC	285	4,425
1879-O	35.00	75.00
1879-S reverse of 1878	35.00	125
1879-S reverse of 1879	35.00	50.00
1880	35.00	45.00
1880-CC reverse of 1878	245	575

	VF	MS-60
1880-CC reverse of 1879	240	480
1880-O	35.00	65.00
1880-S	35.00	45.00
1881	35.00	50.00
1881-CC	410	540
1881-O	35.00	45.00
1881-S	35.00	45.00
1882	35.00	45.00
1882-CC	110	190
1882-O	35.00	50.00
1882-S	35.00	45.00
1883	35.00	50.00
1883-CC	110	200
1883-O	35.00	45.00
1883-S	40.00	625
1884	35.00	45.00
1884-CC	140	200
1884-O	35.00	45.00
1884-S	35.00	7,500
1885	35.00	45.00
1885-CC	580	615
1885-O	35.00	45.00
1885-S	40.00	245
1886	35.00	45.00
1886-O	35.00	685
1886-S	85.00	325
1887	35.00	45.00
1887-O	35.00	50.00
1887-S	40.00	130

	VF	MS-60
1888	35.00	45.00
1888-O	35.00	45.00
1888-S	210	300
1889	35.00	45.00
1889-CC	1,265	23,000
1889-O	35.00	140
1889-S	65.00	210
1890	35.00	45.00
1890-CC	100	440
1890-O	35.00	70.00
1890-S	35.00	60.00
1891	35.00	55.00
1891-CC	100	365
1891-O	35.00	145
1891-S	35.00	55.00
1892	40.00	145
1892-CC	290	1,485
1892-O	40.00	155
1892-S	135	44,500
1893	260	700
1893-CC	625	4,000
1893-O	380	2,525
1893-S	5,700	102,500
1894	1,550	3,500
1894-O	60.00	630
1894-S	110	785
1895 proof	36,500	—
1895-O	480	15,500
1895-S	935	3,850

	VF	MS-60
1896	35.00	45.00
1896-O	35.00	1,450
1896-S	60.00	1,775
1897	35.00	45.00
1897-O	35.00	735
1897-S	35.00	65.00
1898	35.00	45.00
1898-O	35.00	45.00
1898-S	35.00	250
1899	215	300
1899-O	35.00	45.00
1899-S	40.00	380
1900	35.00	45.00
1900-O	35.00	45.00
1900-S	40.00	320

	VF	MS-60
1901	60.00	2,350
1901-O	35.00	45.00
1901-S	30.00	470
1902	35.00	45.00
1902-O	35.00	45.00
1902-S	160	425
1903	55.00	75.00
1903-O	375	410
1903-S	215	3,950
1904	35.00	80.00
1904-O	35.00	50.00
1904-S	90.00	1,225
1921	35.00	45.00
1921-D	35.00	45.00
1921-S	35.00	45.00

PEACE

Like the Morgan dollar before it, the Peace dollar was the result of a congressional mandate for a new, large coinage of silver dollars. When the coin collecting community learned of plans for a new silver dollar, it pushed for a new design to commemorate the end of World War I rather than reviving the Morgan dollar design. The new design by sculptor Anthony de Francisci depicts a radiant Liberty head on the obverse. The reverse depicts an eagle on a rocky perch above the word "Peace."

Like the Morgan dollar, large numbers of Peace dollars survived, particularly in uncirculated grades. Though popular as classic U.S. silver dollars, they are not as popular as Morgan dollars among collectors and investors. As a result, they are more affordable in higher grades.

Size: 38.1 millimeters. **Weight:** 26.73 grams.
Composition: 90 percent silver (0.7736 troy ounces), 10 percent copper.

	VF	MS-60
1921	135	260
1922	30.00	40.00
1922-D	30.00	40.00
1922-S	30.00	45.00
1923	30.00	40.00
1923-D	30.00	50.00
1923-S	30.00	40.00
1924	30.00	40.00
1924-S	35.00	190
1925	30.00	45.00
1925-S	35.00	75.00
1926	30.00	40.00
1926-D	30.00	65.00

	VF	MS-60
1926-S	30.00	45.00
1927	35.00	70.00
1927-D	35.00	170
1927-S	35.00	170
1928	400	500
1928-S large S	50.00	220
1928-S small S	30.00	170
1934	35.00	120
1934-D	35.00	160
1934-S	80.00	1,800
1935	35.00	65.00
1935-S	35.00	250

Clad dollars

EISENHOWER

Dwight D. Eisenhower, supreme commander of the Allied forces in Europe during World War II and the 34th U.S. president, died March 28, 1969. Legislation to again strike a dollar coin, which had not been produced since 1935, was introduced in Congress the following fall. It stated that Eisenhower be honored on the dollar's obverse. The reverse was to be emblematic of the first moon landing, which occurred July 20, 1969.

U.S. Mint Chief Sculptor-Engraver Frank Gasparro designed both sides of the coin. For the reverse, Gasparro fashioned an eagle with an olive branch, a symbol of peace, in its claws landing on the moon with the Earth symbolized as a small orb in the background. The Apollo 11 spacecraft that first landed on the moon was nicknamed "The Eagle."

The Eisenhower dollar legislation also authorized the production of 40 percent silver specimens for inclusion in mint and proof sets.

Size: *38.1 millimeters.* **Weight:** *24.59 grams (silver issues) and 22.68 grams (copper-nickel issues).* **Clad composition:** *75 percent copper and 25 percent nickel bonded to a pure copper core.* **Silver clad composition:** *Clad layers of 80 percent silver and 20 percent copper bonded to a core of 20.9 percent silver and 79.1 percent copper (0.3161 total troy ounces of silver).*

	MS-63	PF-65
1971	10.00	—
1971-D	8.00	—
1971-S silver	16.00	11.00
1972	18.00	—
1972-D	9.00	—
1972-S silver	16.00	10.00
1973	12.00	—

	MS-63	PF-65
1973-D	12.00	—
1973-S	—	12.00
1973-S silver	16.00	45.00
1974	15.00	—
1974-D	7.50	—
1974-S	—	11.00
1974-S silver	16.00	11.00

Bicentennial reverse

A variety of coinage proposals for the nation's bicentennial emerged in the years leading up to the celebration. Among them were proposals for special commemorative coins (the U.S. Mint had not issued commemorative coins since 1954), redesigning all six circulating coins, issuing a two-cent coin with a Bicentennial design, and issuing a gold commemorative coin. The Mint and Treasury Department initially resisted any changes to circulating coin designs and the issuance of commemorative coins, but they eased their opposition as the various proposals were winnowed to a final bill that was signed into law Oct. 18, 1973, by President Richard M. Nixon. That bill called for quarters, half dollars, and dollar coins struck after July 4, 1975, to bear new reverse designs emblematic of the nation's Bicentennial. The law also called for the coins to bear the dual date "1776-1976."

The law also authorized the Mint to strike the Bicentennial coins in a 40 percent silver composition for inclusion in three-coin mint and proof sets for sale directly to collectors.

To select designs for the Bicentennial coins, the Mint sponsored a contest open to all U.S. citizens. A depiction of the Liberty Bell superimposed over the moon, submitted by Dennis R. Williams of Columbus, Ohio, was selected for the dollar.

Notes: *In 1976 the lettering on the reverse was changed to thinner letters, resulting in Type 1 (thicker letters) and Type 2 (thinner letters) for that year.*

	MS-63	PF-65
1976 Type 1	12.00	—
1976 Type 2	8.00	—
1976-D Type 1	7.50	—
1976-D Type 2	6.00	—

	MS-63	PF-65
1976-S Type 1	—	10.00
1976-S Type 2	—	9.00
1976-S silver	16.00	14.00

Regular reverse resumed

	MS-63	PF-65
1977	5.00	—
1977-D	4.00	—
1977-S	—	9.00

	MS-63	PF-65
1978	4.00	—
1978-D	4.75	—
1978-S	—	9.00

ANTHONY

The U.S. government attempted to reverse the public's rejection of circulating dollar coins when it authorized a new, smaller dollar coin in legislation signed into law by President Jimmy Carter on Oct. 10, 1978. The law specified that the coin's obverse honor 19th-century women's activist Susan B. Anthony (1820-1906). U.S. Mint Chief Sculptor-Engraver Frank Gasparro designed the obverse profile of Anthony. The reverse adapted Gasparro's design of an eagle landing on the moon used on the Eisenhower dollar.

Through 1980, the Mint struck more than 847 million Anthony dollars, but by 1981, many of them sat in Mint storage because banks were not ordering them. Thus, the Mint struck 1981-dated Anthony dollars for mint and proof sets only, and stopped production altogether after 1981.

In the 1990s, however, mass-transit organizations and the vending-machine industry started drawing down the government's inventory of Anthony dollars as their automated systems started accepting the higher denomination. As a result, the Mint struck more than 41 million 1999 Anthony dollars.

Size: *26.5 millimeters.* **Weight:** *8.1 grams.* **Composition:** *Clad layers of 75 percent copper and 25 percent nickel bonded to a pure copper core.* **Notes:** *The 1979-S and 1981-S Type 2 coins have a clearer mintmark than the Type 1 varieties for those years.*

	MS-63	PF-65
1979-P	2.50	—
1979-D	3.00	—
1979-S	3.00	—
1979-S Type 1	—	8.00
1979-S Type 2	—	110
1980-P	3.00	—
1980-D	3.00	—
1980-S	3.50	8.00

	MS-63	PF-65
1981-P	7.50	—
1981-D	7.50	—
1981-S	7.50	—
1981-S Type 1	—	8.00
1981-S Type 2	—	230
1999-P	4.00	25.00
1999-D	4.00	—

SACAGAWEA

The Sacagawea dollar is yet another attempt to get U.S. consumers to use a circulating dollar coin. Its authorizing legislation attempted to correct the objections to the Anthony dollar, which was often confused with the quarter. To make it more distinctive, the Sacagawea dollar has a golden color, a plain edge instead of a reeded edge, and a wider border around its design than other circulating coins have.

The authorizing law did not mandate a design theme for the coin. That was left to Treasury Secretary Robert E. Rubin, who created the Dollar Coin Design Advisory Committee to lead the process. With public input, the citizen panel eventually recommended a design featuring Sacagawea, the Native American woman who accompanied Lewis and Clark on their exploration of the American West.

Diameter: *26.4 millimeters.* **Weight:** *8.07 grams.* **Composition:** *88.5 percent copper, 6 percent zinc, 3.5 percent manganese, 2 percent nickel.*

	MS-63	PF-65
2000-P	2.00	—
2000-D	2.00	—
2000-S	—	10.00
2001-P	2.00	—
2001-D	2.00	—
2001-S	—	100.00
2002-P	2.00	—
2002-D	2.00	—
2002-S	—	28.50
2003-P	3.00	—
2003-D	3.00	—
2003-S	—	20.00
2004-P	2.50	—
2004-D	2.50	—

	MS-63	PF-65
2004-S	—	22.50
2005-P	2.50	—
2005-D	2.50	—
2005-S	—	22.50
2006-P	2.50	—
2006-D	5.00	—
2006-S	—	22.50
2007-P	2.50	—
2007-D	2.50	—
2007-S	—	22.50
2008-P	2.50	—
2008-D	2.50	—
2008-S	—	22.50

NATIVE AMERICAN

The Native American $1 Coin Act, passed in 2007, mandated that the reverse of the Sacagawea dollar coin be changed each year beginning in 2009 to celebrate the contributions of Indian tribes and individual Native Americans to the country's development and history. The coins' obverses will continue to depict Sacagawea. The date of issue, mintmark, and motto "E Pluribus Unum" appear as incused lettering on the edges of the Native American dollars. The coins are struck in the same specifications as the original Sacagawea dollar coins.

	Agriculture	MS-63	PF-65
	2009-P	2.00	—
	2009-D	2.00	—
	2009-S	—	22.50
	Great Tree of Peace	MS-63	PF-65
	2010-P	2.00	—
	2010-D	2.00	—
	2010-S	—	22.50
	Diplomacy, Treaties with Tribal Nations	MS-63	PF-65
	2011-P	2.00	—
	2011-D	2.00	—
	2011-S	—	8.00
	17th-century Trade Routes	MS-63	PF-65
	2012-P	—	—
	2012-D	—	—
	2012-S	—	—

The Presidential $1 Coin Act of 2005 cites a Government Accountability Office study that says Americans would use dollar coins if they were struck with attractive, educational, and rotating designs, like the 50 State quarters. But in December 2011, Treasury Secretary Timothy F. Geithner announced that the U.S. Mint would suspend production of Presidential dollars for circulation because of a large backlog of inventory. Geithner said collectors could continue to purchase future issues in the series from the Mint.

Four presidents will be honored each year through 2015 in the order in which served. The program is scheduled to conclude in 2016 with issues honoring Richard M. Nixon and Gerald Ford. The law specifies that a former or current president cannot be added to the series while he is still alive or within two years of his death.

The law mandates that the coins' obverses depict a likeness of the president being honored, his name, a number indicating the order in which he served, and the years of his term or terms. Grover Cleveland, the only president to serve two non-consecutive terms (1885-1889 and 1893-1897), appears on two separate coins in 2012 as the 22nd and 24th president.

The law designates that the common reverse design be a depiction of the Statue of Liberty.

Diameter: *26.4 millimeters.* **Weight:** *8.07 grams.* **Composition:** *88.5 percent copper, 6 percent zinc, 3.5 percent manganese, 2 percent nickel.*

Washington	MS-63	PF-65
2007-P	2.00	—
2007-D	2.00	—
2007-S	—	8.00

J. Adams	MS-63	PF-65
2007-P	2.00	—
2007-D	2.00	—
2007-S	—	8.00

Jefferson	MS-63	PF-65
2007-P	2.00	—
2007-D	2.00	—
2007-S	—	8.00

Madison	MS-63	PF-65
2007-P	2.00	—
2007-D	2.00	—
2007-S	—	8.00

Monroe	MS-63	PF-65
2008-P	2.00	—
2008-D	2.00	—
2008-S	—	8.00

J.Q. Adams	MS-63	PF-65
2008-P	2.00	—
2008-D	2.00	—
2008-S	—	8.00

Jackson	MS-63	PF-65
2008-P	2.00	—
2008-D	2.00	—
2008-S	—	8.00

Van Buren	MS-63	PF-65
2008-P	2.00	—
2008-D	2.00	—
2008-S	—	8.00

Harrison	MS-63	PF-65
2009-P	2.00	—
2009-D	2.00	—
2009-S	—	8.00

Tyler	MS-63	PF-65
2009-P	2.00	—
2009-D	2.00	—
2009-S	—	8.00

Polk	MS-63	PF-65
2009-P	2.00	—
2009-D	2.00	—
2009-S	—	8.00

Taylor	MS-63	PF-65
2009-P	2.00	—
2009-D	2.00	—
2009-S	—	8.00

Fillmore	MS-63	PF-65
2010-P	2.00	—
2010-D	2.00	—
2010-S	—	8.00

Pierce	MS-63	PF-65
2010-P	2.00	—
2010-D	2.00	—
2010-S	—	8.00

Buchanan	MS-63	PF-65
2010-P	2.00	—
2010-D	2.00	—
2010-S	—	8.00

Lincoln	MS-63	PF-65
2010-P	2.00	—
2010-D	2.00	—
2010-S	—	8.00

A. Johnson	MS-63	PF-65
2011-P	2.00	—
2011-D	2.00	—
2011-S	—	8.00

Grant	MS-63	PF-65
2011-P	2.00	—
2011-D	2.00	—
2011-S	—	8.00

Hayes	MS-63	PF-65
2011-P	2.00	—
2011-D	2.00	—
2011-S	—	8.00

Garfield	MS-63	PF-65
2011-P	2.00	—
2011-D	2.00	—
2011-S	—	8.00

Arthur	MS-63	PF-65
2012-P	—	—
2012-D	—	—
2012-S	—	—

Cleveland 1	MS-63	PF-65
2012-P	—	—
2012-D	—	—
2012-S	—	—

Harrison	MS-63	PF-65
2012-P	—	—
2012-D	—	—
2012-S	—	—

Cleveland 2	MS-63	PF-65
2012-P	—	—
2012-D	—	—
2012-S	—	—

Gold dollars

A gold dollar coin was included in legislation proposed in 1836 but was opposed by U.S. Mint Director Robert Patterson and was dropped from the final bill. Patterson thought the coin's physical size was too small and had patterns struck apparently to illustrate his point. A gold dollar coin was proposed again in 1844. Patterson again had patterns produced, from the same dies used for the 1836 patterns, and again opposed the coin. He said small gold coins in general were not popular. A congressional committee failed to approve the 1844 proposal.

A bill authorizing a gold dollar coin reappeared in early 1849 after gold was discovered in California in late 1848. Authorization of a gold $20 coin was added to the bill later. Patterson and others continued to object to a gold dollar coin because of its small size, but the legislation passed on March 3, 1849.

The gold dollar's diameter was stretched 2 millimeters in 1854 (Type 2), but the total weight and gold content remained the same. The change was accompanied by some design modifications, which included adding an Indian headdress to the portrait of Liberty on the obverse. The design was further tweaked in 1856 (Type 3).

TYPE 1

Size: *13 millimeters.* **Weight:** *1.672 grams.*
Composition: *90 percent gold (0.0484 troy ounces), 10 percent copper.*

	VF	XF
1849	225	265
1849-C	950	1,450
1849-D	1,300	1,875
1849-O	235	310
1850	210	245
1850-C	1,150	1,600

	VF	XF
1850-D	1,250	1,725
1850-O	275	390
1851	210	245
1851-C	1,150	1,500
1851-D	1,250	1,675
1851-O	195	240

	VF	XF
1852	210	245
1852-C	1,040	1,400
1852-D	1,250	1,675
1852-O	175	260
1853	210	245
1853-C	1,100	1,400

	VF	XF
1853-D	1,250	1,700
1853-O	160	235
1854	210	245
1854-D	1,400	2,350
1854-S	360	525

TYPE 2

Size: *15 millimeters.* **Weight:** *1.672 grams.*
Composition: *90 percent gold (0.0484 ounces), 10 percent copper.*

	VF	XF
1854	280	410
1855	280	410
1855-C	1,450	3,750

	VF	XF
1855-D	4,750	9,800
1855-O	440	600
1856-S	820	1,325

TYPE 3

Size: *15 millimeters.* **Weight:** *1.672 grams.*
Composition: *90 percent gold (0.0484 ounces), 10 percent copper.*

	VF	XF
1856	250	285
1856-D	3,650	5,800
1857	245	285

	VF	XF
1857-C	1,150	1,750
1857-D	1,300	2,300
1857-S	520	650

	VF	XF
1858	245	285
1858-D	1,250	1,600
1858-S	400	575
1859	245	285
1859-C	1,050	1,700
1859-D	1,500	2,100
1859-S	265	525
1860	245	285
1860-D	2,500	4,200
1860-S	380	500
1861	245	285
1861-D	7,000	11,000
1862	245	285
1863	500	925
1864	370	475
1865	370	590
1866	385	470
1867	420	525
1868	290	415
1869	460	530
1870	290	410

	VF	XF
1870-S	475	785
1871	290	390
1872	300	400
1873 closed 3	425	825
1873 open 3	245	285
1874	245	285
1875	2,350	4,650
1876	300	360
1877	210	340
1878	250	365
1879	225	285
1880	265	300
1881	270	300
1882	275	300
1883	365	300
1884	265	300
1885	265	300
1886	265	300
1887	265	300
1888	265	300
1889	265	300

Gold $2.50

LIBERTY CAP

Authorization for a gold $2.50 coin, or quarter eagle, was part of the original U.S. Mint act, passed April 2, 1792. Early proposals by Alexander Hamilton, Thomas Jefferson, and others had included only $5 or $10 coins, or both, but Congress added the $2.50 coin.

The Liberty Cap type, designed by Robert Scot, features Liberty wearing a tall conical cap. The Liberty Cap gold $2.50 was the first U.S. coin to depict a heraldic eagle with a shield on its chest.

Size: *20 millimeters.* **Weight:** *4.37 grams.*
Composition: *91.67 percent gold (0.1289 troy ounces), 8.33 percent copper.*

	F	XF
1796 no stars on obverse	55,000	100,000
1796 stars on obverse	26,500	65,000
1797	20,000	45,000
1798	5,250	15,500
1802	4,250	14,500

	F	XF
1804 13 stars on reverse	45,000	125,000
1804 14 stars on reverse	4,550	15,500
1805	4,250	14,500
1806	4,250	15,000
1807	4,250	14,500

TURBAN HEAD

A redesign in 1808 turned Liberty around – from right facing to left facing – on the obverse and adorned her in a turban. On the reverse, a more natural-looking eagle and the denomination, "2 1/2 D.", was added. After just one year of production, however, the U.S. Mint turned its attention to producing low-denomination silver coins rather than gold coins, which were largely exported at a profit.

Gold $2.50 coinage resumed for one year in 1821 and then again in 1824 after gold was discovered in South Carolina that year. The diameter was reduced slightly, but the gold content remained the same. The obverse design was modified, although the basic design concept of a turban-head Liberty was retained. The same reverse design from 1808 was used with minor modification. The design was reduced slightly again in 1829, and the obverse again saw some modification of the basic turban-head concept.

Size: *20 millimeters (1808), 18.5 millimeters (1821-1827), and 18.2 millimeters (1829-1834).* **Composition:** *91.67 percent gold (0.1289 troy ounces), 8.33 percent copper.*

	F	XF
1808	26,500	54,500

	F	XF
1821	5,950	10,350
1824	5,950	10,250
1825	5,950	10,250

	F	XF
1826	6,450	11,000
1827	6,050	10,750

	F	XF
1829	5,400	7,950
1830	5,400	7,950
1831	5,400	7,950

	F	XF
1832	5,400	7,950
1833	5,400	7,950
1834	8,900	15,450

CLASSIC HEAD

Coinage reform legislation passed in 1834 increased the gold-to-silver value ratio in the U.S. bimetallic monetary system from 15-to-1 to 16.002-to-1. Thus, the fineness and gold content of the $2.50 decreased.

A new rendering of Liberty appeared on the obverse; minor design modifications appeared on the reverse.

Size: *18.2 millimeters.* **Weight:** *4.18 grams.*
Composition: *89.92 percent gold (0.1209 troy ounces), 10.08 percent copper.*

	VF	XF
1834	475	675
1835	475	675
1836	475	675
1837	500	800
1838	500	625

	VF	XF
1838-C	1,700	3,000
1839	500	900
1839-C	1,500	2,650
1839-D	1,750	3,450
1839-O	700	1,100

CORONET

Legislation passed in 1837 set the fineness of all U.S. gold and silver coins at 0.9000 and revised the gold-to-silver value ratio to 15.998-to-1. Thus, the size and actual gold weight of the $2.50 coin changed slightly in 1840.

A new image of Liberty, which emulated the one used on higher-denomination gold coins of the time, appeared on the obverse. With some modification, the basic reverse design used since 1808 was retained.

Size: *18 millimeters.* **Weight:** *4.18 grams.*
Composition: *90 percent gold (0.121 troy ounces), 10 percent copper.*

	F	XF		F	XF
1840	160	900	1844-D	785	2,200
1840-C	975	1,600	1845	190	350
1840-D	2,000	8,700	1845-D	950	2,600
1840-O	250	825	1845-O	550	2,300
1841	—	85,000	1846	200	500
1841-C	750	2,000	1846-C	725	3,500
1841-D	950	4,750	1846-D	800	2,000
1842	500	2,600	1846-O	170	400
1842-C	700	3,500	1847	140	360
1842-D	900	4,000	1847-C	900	2,300
1842-O	240	1,200	1847-D	800	2,250
1843	160	450	1847-O	165	400
1843-C	800	2,200	1848	315	850
1843-D	920	2,350	1848-C	800	2,100
1843-O	165	250	1848-D	1,000	2,500
1844	225	850	1849	180	475
1844-C	700	2,600	1849-C	800	2,150

	F	XF
1849-D	950	2,500
1850	265	360
1850-C	800	2,000
1850-D	950	2,350
1850-O	300	485
1851	265	330
1851-C	900	2,250
1851-D	1,000	2,500
1851-O	300	370
1852	265	330
1852-C	975	2,100
1852-D	1,100	2,950
1852-O	300	365
1853	265	330
1853-D	1,250	3,450
1854	265	330
1854-C	1,100	2,450
1854-D	2,100	6,950
1854-O	300	365
1854-S	95,000	300,000
1855	270	335
1855-C	1,050	3,250
1855-D	2,100	7,500
1856	270	335
1856-C	685	2,500
1856-D	3,850	12,850
1856-O	300	750
1856-S	300	425
1857	270	335

	F	XF
1857-D	1,025	2,775
1857-O	300	425
1857-S	300	365
1858	275	340
1858-C	965	2,100
1859	275	350
1859-D	1,150	3,100
1859-S	310	950
1860	275	340
1860-C	985	2,175
1860-S	310	625
1861	270	335
1831-S	320	900
1862	310	600
1862-S	650	2,100
1863 *rare*		
1863-S	465	1,500
1864	3,750	11.500
1865	2,950	7,750
1865-S	320	600
1866	775	3,150
1866-S	365	625
1867	350	850
1867-S	300	575
1868	300	400
1868-S	270	365
1869	300	435
1869-S	300	440
1870	290	550

	F	XF		F	XF
1870-S	270	465	1885	400	1,850
1871	300	385	1886	275	375
1871-S	270	415	1887	275	365
1872	300	800	1888	270	365
1872-S	275	485	1889	270	365
1873	270	365	1890	375	365
1873-S	280	400	1891	275	365
1874	285	425	1892	275	365
1875	1,950	5,500	1893	270	355
1875-S	270	375	1894	275	365
1876	285	675	1895	265	355
1876-S	285	625	1896	265	350
1877	310	875	1897	270	350
1877-S	265	355	1898	265	345
1878	265	345	1899	265	345
1878-S	265	345	1900	265	345
1879	270	355	1901	265	345
1879-S	270	365	1902	265	345
1880	275	385	1903	265	345
1881	950	3,150	1904	265	345
1882	270	375	1905	265	345
1883	280	750	1906	265	345
1884	275	440	1907	265	345

INDIAN HEAD

A new design by Bela Lyon Pratt replaced the long-running Coronet Head in 1908 on the gold $2.50. Its intaglio features were unusual and controversial. Some feared the incuse design would allow dirt and germs to accumulate in the coin's recesses. From a collector's standpoint, however, the technique shielded the coin from wear.

Legislation passed April 11, 1930, discontinued the gold $2.50.

Size: *18 millimeters.* **Weight:** *4.18 grams.*
Composition: *90 percent gold (0.121 troy ounces), 10 percent copper.*

	VF	AU
1908	255	310
1909	255	310
1910	255	310
1911	255	310
1911-D	1,150	2,850
1912	255	315
1913	255	310
1914	260	370

	VF	AU
1914-D	255	320
1915	255	300
1925-D	255	300
1926	255	300
1927	255	300
1928	255	300
1929	255	320

Gold $3

The country's gold interests promoted and achieved authorization for a $3 coin in 1853. U.S. Mint engraver James B. Longacre, who designed the coin, described the denomination as "anomalous" among the gold $1, $2.50, $5, $10, and $20 issues of the time. He struggled with creating a design that would sufficiently distinguish it from the $2.50 coin, which was slightly smaller in physical size. The result depicts Liberty in a feathered tiara on the obverse and a wreath surrounding the denomination, as opposed to the $2.50's eagle, on the reverse.

The gold $3 never caught on with the public and saw little use in circulation. Legislation passed Sept. 26, 1890, discontinued the gold $3 coin.

Size: *20.5 millimeters.* **Weight:** *5.015 grams.*
Composition: *90 percent gold (0.1452 troy ounces), 10 percent copper.*

	VF	XF
1854	850	1,100
1854-D	8,300	15,000
1854-O	1,000	2,000
1855	900	1,100
1855-S	1,025	2,150
1856	880	1,100
1856-S	900	1,500
1857	900	1,100
1857-S	950	2,200
1858	950	1,800
1859	900	1,800
1860	900	1,600
1860-S	950	2,000
1861	925	1,500

	VF	XF
1862	925	1,850
1863	900	1,450
1864	950	1,500
1865	1,350	2,500
1866	970	1,100
1867	950	1,100
1868	740	2,100
1869	1,150	2,200
1870	1,000	1,500
1870-S *1 known*		
1871	1,000	1,500
1872	900	1,800
1873 open 3, *proof*	3,300	5,000

	VF	XF
1873 closed 3	4,000	6,000
1874	800	1,300
1875 *proof*	20,000	28,000
1876	6,000	10,000
1877	1,200	2,900
1878	800	1,300
1879	850	1,300
1880	850	1,700
1881	1,400	2,750

	VF	XF
1882	925	1,400
1883	1,000	1,600
1884	1,250	1,700
1885	1,300	1,800
1886	1,250	1,800
1887	900	1,300
1888	950	1,500
1889	925	1,300

Gold $5

Authorization for a gold $5 coin, or half eagle, was part of the original U.S. Mint act, passed April 2, 1792. It was the first gold coin produced by the fledgling United States. The design emulated the gold $2.50 coin but in a larger size.

There are many design varieties among early dates. They include variations in the number of stars, new dates engraved over old dates on the dies used to strike the coins, and variations in the size of the numbers, letters, and stars in the design.

Small eagle

Size: *25 millimeters.* **Weight:** *8.75 grams.*
Composition: *91.67 gold (0.258 troy ounces), 8.33 percent copper.*

	F	VF
1795	19,500	25,000
1796	20,500	25,350
1797 15 stars	23,000	27,500

	F	VF
1797 16 stars	21,000	25,850
1798	112,000	185,000

Heraldic eagle

In 1795, 1797, and 1798, the Liberty Cap gold $5 was also struck with a heraldic eagle on the reverse. The heraldic-eagle reverse continued to be used after 1798, and the "small eagle" reverse was discontinued.

Size: *25 millimeters.* **Weight:** *8.75 grams.*
Composition: *91.67 gold (0.258 troy ounces), 8.33 percent copper.*

	F	VF
1795	10,000	16,500
1797	10,850	17,500
1798 small 8	4,850	6,650
1798 large 8, 13 reverse stars	4,100	5,100
1798 large 8, 14 reverse stars	5,100	6,650
1799 small reverse stars	3,850	4,900

	F	VF
1799 large reverse stars	3,950	4,750
1800	3,850	4,650
1802	3,850	4,650
1803	3,850	4,650
1804 small 8	3,850	4,650
1804 small 8 over large 8	3,950	4,850
1805	3,850	4,650
1806	3,850	4,650
1807	3,850	4,650

TURBAN HEAD

A redesign turned Liberty around – from right facing to left facing – on the obverse and adorned her in a turban. On the reverse, a more natural-looking eagle and the denomination, "5 D.", was added.

The U.S. Mint continued to strike gold $5 coins despite the suspension of gold $2.50 production from 1809 through 1820 and gold $10 production from 1805 through 1837 to concentrate on the production of small-denomination silver coins.

Capped, draped bust

Size: *25 millimeters.* **Weight:** *8.75 grams.*
Composition: *91.67 percent gold (0.258 troy ounces), 8.33 percent copper.*

	F	VF
1807	3,100	3,850
1808	3,600	4,500
1808	3,100	3,850
1809	3,100	3,850
1810 small date, small 5	17,500	32,500

	F	VF
1810 small date, large 5	3,100	3,850
1810 large date, small 5	17,500	37,500
1810 large date, large 5	3,100	3,850
1811	3,100	3,850
1812	3,100	3,850

Capped bust

Some minor redesign of Liberty on the obverse resulted in the image being shortened to the neckline.

	F	VF
1813	3,100	3,850
1814	5,000	6,250
1815	32,500	50,000
1818	5,000	6,450
1819	8,800	16,500
1820	5,100	6,400
1821	12,000	22,000
1822 *3 known*		
1823	5,500	6,250
1824	5,500	10,500
1825	5,500	9,500
1826	5,500	7,800
1827	6,000	10,000

	F	VF
1828	6,000	13,000
1829 large planchet	15,000	28,500
1829 small planchet	37,500	54,000
1830	16,500	27,500
1831	16,500	27,500
1832 curved-base 2, 12 stars	50,000	80,000
1832 square-base 2, 13 stars	16,500	27,500
1833	16,500	27,500
1834	17,000	29,000

CLASSIC HEAD

Coinage reform legislation passed in 1834 increased the gold-to-silver value ratio in the U.S. bimetallic monetary system from 15-to-1 to 16.002-to-1. Thus, the fineness and gold content of the $5 decreased. The value of the gold content of the previous $5 coins had exceeded their face value.

Obverse and reverse designs were also modified slightly. Most notably, the motto "E Pluribus Unum" was removed from the reverse to distinguish the new coins from the old ones.

Size: *22.5 millimeters.* **Weight:** *8.36 grams.*
Composition: *89.92 percent gold (0.2416 troy ounces), 10.08 percent copper.*

	VF	XF
1834 plain 4	550	790
1834 crosslet 4	1,650	2,900
1835	550	790
1836	550	790

	VF	XF
1837	550	790
1838	550	890
1838-C	2,550	5,500
1838-D	2,100	4,650

CORONET

Legislation passed in 1837 set the fineness of all U.S. gold and silver coins at 0.9000 and revised the gold-to-silver value ratio to 15.998-to-1. Thus, the diameter and actual gold weight of the $5 coin changed slightly in 1839.

A new image of Liberty appeared on the obverse. With some modification, the basic reverse design used since 1807 was retained.

Size: *21.6 millimeters.* **Weight:** *8.359 grams.*
Composition: *90 percent gold (0.242 troy ounces), 10 percent copper.*

	VF	XF
1839	560	590
1839-C	2,300	2,900
1839-D	2,200	3,200
1840	550	570
1840-C	2,200	3,000
1840-D	2,200	3,000
1840-O	580	610
1841	560	590
1841-C	1,850	2,400
1841-D	1,800	2,350
1841-O *2 known*		
1842 small letters	410	1,100
1842 large letters	750	2,000
1842-C	1,800	2,200

	VF	XF
1842-D small date	2,000	2,300
1842-D large date	2,350	6,500
1842-O	1,000	3,400
1843	550	580
1843-C	1,850	2,500
1843-D	1,950	2,600
1843-O small letters	580	1,700
1843-O large letters	585	1,175
1844	550	580
1844-C	1,900	3,000
1844-D	1,950	2,400
1844-O	585	590
1845	550	580

	VF	XF
1845-D	1,900	2,400
1845-O	415	800
1846	550	580
1846-C	1,900	3,000
1846-D	1,800	2,400
1846-O	410	1,000
1847	550	580
1847-C	1,800	2,400
1847-D	2,000	2,500
1847-O	2,200	6,750
1848	550	580
1848-C	1,900	2,250
1848-D	2,000	2,350
1849	550	580
1849-C	1,900	2,400
1849-D	2,000	2,600
1850	550	580
1850-C	1,850	2,300
1850-D	1,950	2,500
1851	550	580
1851-C	1,900	2,350
1851-D	1,950	2,400
1851-O	600	1,500
1852	550	580
1852-C	1,900	2,450
1852-D	2,000	2,450
1853	550	580
1853-C	1,950	2,350
1853-D	2,000	2,500

	VF	XF
1854	550	580
1854-C	1,900	2,300
1854-D	1,875	2,200
1854-O	580	610
1854-S *rare*		
1855	550	580
1855-C	1,900	2,300
1855-D	1,950	2,400
1855-O	675	2,100
1855-S	410	1,000
1856	550	580
1856-C	1,875	2,400
1856-D	1,950	2,600
1856-O	650	1,600
1856-S	410	590
1857	550	580
1857-C	1,900	2,500
1857-D	2,000	2,650
1857-O	640	1,400
1857-S	560	590
1858	560	590
1858-C	1,900	2,350
1858-D	2,000	2,450
1858-S	825	2,350
1859	560	590
1859-C	1,900	2,450
1859-D	2,150	2,600
1859-S	1,800	4,150
1860	560	590

	VF	XF
1860-C	2,100	3,000
1860-D	1,900	2,600
1860-S	1,100	2,100
1861	550	590
1861-C	2,400	3,900
1861-D	4,700	7,000
1861-S	1,100	4,500
1862	800	1,850

	VF	XF
1862-S	3,000	6,000
1863	1,200	3,750
1863-S	1,450	4,100
1864	650	1,850
1864-S	4,750	16,000
1865	1,450	4,100
1865-S	1,400	2,400
1866-S	1,750	4,000

Motto above eagle

A congressional act passed March 3, 1865, allowed the addition of the motto "In God We Trust" to all U.S. gold and silver coins.

	VF	XF
1866	750	1,650
1866-S	900	2,600
1867	500	1,500
1867-S	1,400	2,900
1868	650	1,000
1868-S	485	1,550
1869	925	2,400
1869-S	500	1,750
1870	800	2,000
1870-CC	5,250	15,000
1870-S	950	2,600

	VF	XF
1871	900	1,700
1871-CC	1,250	3,000
1871-S	500	950
1872	850	1,925
1872-CC	1,250	5,000
1872-S	535	800
1873 closed 3	470	485
1873 open 3	465	475
1873-CC	2,600	12,500
1873-S	525	1,400
1874	660	1,675

	VF	XF		VF	XF
1874-CC	850	1,700	1884	480	500
1874-S	640	2,100	1884-CC	625	975
1875	34,000	45,000	1884-S	480	490
1875-CC	1,400	4,500	1885	460	470
1875-S	715	2,250	1885-S	460	470
1876	1,100	2,500	1886	460	470
1876-CC	1,450	5,000	1886-S	460	470
1876-S	2,000	3,600	1887	—	14,500
1877	900	2,750	1887-S	460	470
1877-CC	1,000	3,300	1888	480	485
1877-S	500	650	1888-S	465	475
1878	470	480	1889	575	585
1878-CC	3,100	7,200	1890	500	510
1878-S	465	475	1890-CC	575	585
1879	465	475	1891	470	480
1879-CC	1,000	1,500	1891-CC	560	565
1879-S	470	480	1892	460	470
1880	460	470	1892-CC	560	585
1880-CC	625	815	1892-O	525	1,000
1880-S	460	470	1892-S	460	470
1881	460	470	1893	460	470
1881-CC	650	1,500	1893-CC	600	635
1881-S	460	470	1893-O	475	580
1882	460	470	1893-S	460	470
1882-CC	625	675	1894	460	470
1882-S	460	470	1894-O	480	490
1883	480	490	1894-S	490	525
1883-CC	625	1,100	1895	460	470
1883-S	480	500	1895-S	470	490

	VF	XF
1896	460	470
1896-S	470	480
1897	460	470
1897-S	460	470
1898	460	470
1898-S	460	470
1899	460	470
1899-S	460	470
1900	460	470
1900-S	460	470
1901	460	470
1901-S	460	470
1902	460	470

	VF	XF
1902-S	460	470
1903	460	470
1903-S	460	470
1904	460	470
1904-S	470	480
1905	460	470
1905-S	460	470
1906	460	470
1906-D	460	470
1906-S	460	470
1907	460	470
1907-D	460	470
1908	460	470

INDIAN HEAD

A new design by Bela Lyon Pratt replaced the long-running Coronet Head in 1908 on the gold $5. Its intaglio features were unusual and controversial. Some feared the incuse design would allow dirt and germs to accumulate in the coin's recesses. From a collector's standpoint, however, the technique shielded the coin from wear.

The Gold Reserve Act of Jan. 30, 1934, discontinued all U.S. gold coinage.

Size: *21.6 millimeters.* **Weight:** *8.359 grams.*
Composition: *90 percent gold (0.242 troy ounces), 10 percent copper.*

	VF	XF
1908	520	530
1908-D	520	530
1908-S	595	605
1909	520	530
1909-D	520	530
1909-O	3,950	4,850
1909-S	550	570
1910	520	530
1910-D	520	530
1910-S	560	585
1911	520	530
1911-D	600	775

	VF	XF
1911-S	530	565
1912	520	530
1912-S	565	595
1913	520	485
1913-S	560	590
1914	520	530
1914-D	520	530
1914-S	565	585
1915	520	530
1915-S	575	605
1916-S	545	565
1929	11,000	14,250

Gold $10

LIBERTY CAP

Authorization for a gold $10 coin, or eagle, was part of the original U.S. Mint act, passed April 2, 1792. The Continental Congress also included a gold $10 coin in its failed attempt to establish a mint and coinage in 1786.

President George Washington received the first example of this coin, struck in 1795. The obverse design emulated the gold $2.50 and $5 coins but in a larger size. On the reverse, only the "small eagle" design was used during the first two years of production.

Early eagles were struck on a primitive screw press with hand-engraved dies, no two of which were identical. The result is numerous variations in design details and coins that were struck from dies with new dates engraved over old dates. Also, many early gold $10 coins have "adjustment marks," which resulted from scraping excess metal off the imperfect planchets. Although coins with adjustment marks are not desirable, they are not considered damaged because the marks were part of the manufacturing process.

The initial issue of 1795-1804 was widely exported and melted because it was undervalued relative to its gold content, particularly by European standards. As a result, eagle production was suspended for more than 30 years.

Small eagle

Size: *33 millimeters.* **Weight:** *17.5 grams.*
Composition: *91.67 percent (0.5159 troy ounces), 8.33 percent copper.*

	F	VF
1795	28,500	33,850
1796	27,500	36,000
1797	31,500	40,000

	F	VF
1797	9,800	12,850
1798 9 stars left, 4 right	13,500	19,000
1798 7 stars left, 6 right	28,500	38,500
1799	9,350	10,750

	F	VF
1800	9,500	10,750
1801	9,250	10,900
1803	9,500	11,500
1804	16,500	22,750

CORONET

The discovery of gold in Southern states and later in California prompted the resumption of $10 coin production in 1838. Legislation passed in 1837 set the fineness of all U.S. gold and silver coins at 0.9000 and revised the gold-to-silver ratio to 15.998-to-1. Thus, the diameter and actual gold weight of the new $10 coin decreased from the previous issue.

The new obverse design, by Christian Gobrecht, featured a portrait of Liberty facing left and wearing a coronet. The reverse featured a new eagle design and, for the first time, the denomination, designated as "Ten D.".

Old-style head

Size: *27 millimeters.* **Weight:** *16.718 grams.*
Composition: *90 percent gold (0.4839 troy ounces), 10 percent copper.*

	F	VF
1838	1,750	2,650

	F	VF
1839	1,150	2,150

New-style head

Some minor redesign of Liberty on the obverse resulted in the image being tilted backward.

	VF	XF
1839	1,550	6,850
1840	1,060	1,335
1841	1,050	1,235
1841-O	3,450	6,950
1842	1,050	1,150
1842-O	1,060	1,465
1843	1,050	1,265
1843-O	1,060	1,220
1844	1,350	3.200
1844-O	1,060	1,400
1845	1,220	1,345
1845-O	1,060	1,335
1846	1,050	1,250
1846-O	1,060	1,150
1847	1,050	1,100
1847-O	1,050	1,100
1848	1,050	1,160
1848-O	1,240	1,850
1849	1,050	1,100

	VF	XF
1849-O	1,240	2,450
1850 large date	1,050	1,100
1850 small date	1,240	2,150
1850-O	1,075	1,275
1851	1,050	1,100
1851-O	1,060	1,150
1852	1,050	1,100
1852-O	1,220	1,650
1853	1,060	1,100
1853-O	1,075	1,160
1854	1,050	1,120
1854-O small date	1,075	1,400
1854-O large date	1,215	2,000
1854-S	1,050	1,120
1855	1,050	1,100
1855-O	1,075	2,100
1856	1,050	1,100

	VF	XF
1856-O	1,375	2,150
1856-S	1,050	1,170
1857	1,075	1,150
1857-O	1,800	3,650
1857-S	1,060	1,100
1858	5,200	8,250
1858-O	1,050	1,420
1858-S	1,600	3,950
1859	1,075	1,280
1859-O	4,250	10,500
1859-S	2,600	5,250
1860	1,115	1,330
1860-O	1,215	1,850

	VF	XF
1860-S	2,950	6,400
1861	1,050	1,100
1861-S	1,600	3,750
1862	1,200	1,300
1862-S	2,000	3,450
1863	4,000	10,000
1863-S	1,600	3,750
1864	1,800	4,950
1864-S	5,100	17,500
1865	1,950	4,850
1865-S	4,850	12,500
1866-S	2,650	5,950

Motto above eagle

A congressional act passed March 3, 1865, allowed the addition of the motto "In God We Trust" to all U.S. gold and silver coins.

	VF	XF		VF	XF
1866	850	2,450	1874-CC	1,150	3,650
1866-S	1,550	3,850	1874-S	1,275	3,400
1867	1,500	2,600	1875	40,000	67,500
1867-S	2,350	6,650	1875-CC	4,250	9,850
1868	1,000	1,100	1876	3,000	8,500
1868-S	1,350	2,400	1876-CC	3,600	7,750
1869	1,550	3,000	1876-S	1,300	2,950
1869-S	1,500	2,700	1877	3,350	6,350
1870	985	1,650	1877-CC	2,400	6,750
1870-CC	13,000	30,000	1877-S	935	1,250
1870-S	1,150	2,850	1878	925	965
1871	1,500	3,000	1878-CC	3,850	10,000
1871-CC	2,600	6,400	1878-S	945	975
1871-S	1,300	2,200	1879	930	965
1872	2,400	5,500	1879-CC	6,650	12,500
1872-CC	2,850	9,850	1879-O	2,150	5,450
1872-S	850	1,175	1879-S	630	965
1873	4,500	9,750	1880	910	930
1873-CC	6,000	13,500	1880-CC	900	1,000
1873-S	1,150	2,850	1880-O	1,030	1,450
1874	935	965	1880-S	910	930

	VF	XF		VF	XF
1881	910	930	1892	910	930
1881-CC	1,055	1,200	1892-CC	1,050	1,100
1881-O	1,000	1,150	1892-O	965	970
1881-S	910	930	1892-S	935	990
1882	910	930	1893	910	930
1882-CC	985	1,750	1893-CC	1,050	1,150
1882-O	940	1,115	1893-O	935	965
1882-S	940	965	1893-S	935	965
1883	910	930	1894	910	930
1883-CC	1,110	1,250	1894-O	935	965
1883-O	3,000	7,950	1894-S	935	990
1883-S	940	965	1895	910	930
1884	940	965	1895-O	935	970
1884-CC	1,130	1,450	1895-S	935	980
1884-S	910	930	1896	910	930
1885	910	930	1896-S	935	960
1885-S	910	930	1897	910	930
1886	910	930	1897-O	935	970
1886-S	910	930	1897-S	935	960
1887	940	965	1898	910	930
1887-S	910	930	1898-S	935	960
1888	940	965	1899	910	930
1888-O	940	965	1899-S	910	930
1888-S	910	930	1899-O	935	965
1889	965	1,155	1900	910	930
1889-S	910	930	1900-S	935	965
1890	950	965	1901	910	930
1890-CC	1,050	1,150	1901-O	935	965
1891	965	1,000	1901-S	910	930
1891-CC	1,050	1,100	1902	910	930

	VF	XF
1902-S	910	930
1903	910	930
1903-O	935	965
1903-S	910	930
1904	910	930
1904-D	935	965
1905	910	930
1905-S	935	960

	VF	XF
1906	910	930
1906-D	910	930
1906-O	935	965
1906-S	935	960
1907	910	930
1907-D	910	930
1907-S	935	960

INDIAN HEAD

Sculptor Augustus Saint-Gaudens designed President Theodore Roosevelt's inaugural medal. Roosevelt liked the result so much that he commissioned the sculptor to improve the design of U.S. coinage. The results included a striking new design, featuring Liberty in an Indian headdress, for the gold $10 coin in 1907. The smooth edge has 46 stars on it, one for each state in the Union at the time. Two more stars were added in 1912.

Size: *27 millimeters.* **Weight:** *16.718 grams.*
Composition: *90 percent gold (0.4839 troy ounces), 10 percent copper.*

	VF	XF
1907 wire edge	13,850	17,500
1907 rolled edge	26,000	38,500

	VF	XF
1907 no periods in "E Pluribus Unum"	1,000	1,030
1908	990	1,015
1908-D	990	1,015

Congressional acts of March 3, 1865, and Feb. 12, 1873, allowed the motto "In God We Trust" to be placed on U.S. coins but did not mandate it. According to author Don Taxay, President Theodore Roosevelt considered it sacrilege to use a religious motto on coinage. When the new 1907 gold $10 and $20 coins appeared without the motto, Congress passed legislation on May 18, 1908, mandating its use on all coins on which it had previously appeared.

The Gold Reserve Act of Jan. 30, 1934, discontinued production of all U.S. gold coinage.

	VF	XF
1908	990	1,000
1908-D	990	1,030
1908-S	1,000	1,065
1909	985	1,000
1909-D	990	1,015
1909-S	990	1,015
1910	985	1,000
1910-D	980	1,000
1910-S	990	1,015
1911	980	1,000
1911-D	1,050	1,200
1911-S	1,020	1,040
1912	985	1,000
1912-S	990	1,015

	VF	XF
1913	985	1,000
1913-S	1,035	1,060
1914	985	1,000
1914-D	985	1,000
1914-S	995	1,020
1915	985	1,000
1915-S	1,035	1,075
1916-S	1,020	1,045
1920-S	12,500	16,850
1926	980	1,000
1930-S	8,500	11,250
1932	980	1,000
1933	—	140,000

FIRST SPOUSE

The Presidential $1 Coin Act of 2005 also authorized the minting of half-ounce gold $10 bullion coins honoring the wives of U.S. presidents. The women will be honored in the order in which they served, and the release schedule parallels the release schedule for the Presidential dollars.

Obverse designs will include the name and likeness of the first spouse, the years during which her husband was president, and a number indicating the order in which her husband served. Reverse images will be emblematic of the spouse's life and work.

For presidents who were not married during their terms in office, the obverse design will include an image of Liberty as depicted on a U.S. coin that circulated during the president's term. Reverse designs will be based on "themes of such President" being honored.

An exception will be the coin for President Chester A. Arthur. The legislation mandates that the obverse depict Alice Paul, a leader in the women's suffrage movement. Paul was born Jan. 11, 1885, during Arthur's term. The reverse design will also represent the suffrage movement.

The First Spouse coins contain a half-ounce of 24-karat gold (.9999 fine).

Diameter: *22 millimeters.* **Weight:** *15.552 grams.*
Composition: *99.99 percent gold (0.4999 troy ounces).*

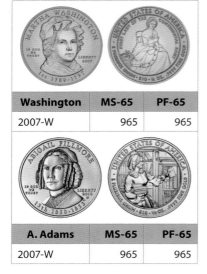

Washington	MS-65	PF-65
2007-W	965	965

A. Adams	MS-65	PF-65
2007-W	965	965

Jefferson	MS-65	PF-65
2007-W	965	965

Madison	MS-65	PF-65
2007-W	965	965

Monroe	MS-65	PF-65
2008-W	1,000	1,075

A. Harrison	MS-65	PF-65
2009-W	1,025	1,000

L. Adams	MS-65	PF-65
2008-W	1,000	985

L. Tyler	MS-65	PF-65
2009-W	1,350	1,450

Jackson	MS-65	PF-65
2008-W	1,275	1,225

J. Tyler	MS-65	PF-65
2009-W	1,500	1,450

Van Buren	MS-65	PF-65
2008-W	1,400	1,350

Polk	MS-65	PF-65
2009-W	935	900

Taylor	MS-65	PF-65
2009-W	855	855

Fillmore	MS-65	PF-65
2010-W	1,025	1,000

Pierce	MS-65	PF-65
2010-W	1,350	1,450

Buchanan	MS-65	PF-65
2010-W	850	850

Lincoln	MS-65	PF-65
2010-W	935	900

E. Johnson	MS-65	PF-65
2011-W	855	855

Grant	MS-65	PF-65
2011-W	855	855

Hayes	MS-65	PF-65
2011-W	950	1,000

Garfield	MS-65	PF-65
2011-W	950	1,000

Paul	MS-65	PF-65
2012-W	—	—

Cleveland 1	MS-65	PF-65
2012-W	—	—

C. Harrison	MS-65	PF-65
2012-W	—	—

Cleveland 2	MS-65	PF-65
2012-W	—	—

Gold $20

LIBERTY

An amendment authorizing a gold $20 coin, or "double eagle," was added to proposed congressional legislation authorizing a gold dollar coin. It passed March 3, 1849. Both coins were advanced by gold interests after the discovery of the precious metal in California in 1848.

James B. Longacre's design for the coin depicts Liberty wearing a coronet, similar to the gold $5 and $10 coins of the same era. The obverse depicts a majestic heraldic eagle with a circle of stars and a radiant arc above it.

Size: *34 millimeters.* **Weight:** *33.436 grams.*
Composition: *90 percent gold (0.9677 troy ounces), 10 percent copper.*

	VF	XF
1849 *1 known*		
1850	1,945	2,025
1850-O	1,880	3,500
1851	1,985	2,155
1851-O	2,060	2,855
1852	1,985	2,155
1852-O	2,015	2,650
1853	1,985	2,155
1853-O	2,075	3,650
1854	1,985	2,155
1854-O	95,000	225,000

	VF	XF
1854-S	2,065	2,145
1855	1,985	2,145
1855-O	3,650	19,500
1855-S	1,965	2,155
1856	1,985	2,155
1856-O	97,500	165,000
1856-S	1,965	2,155
1857	1,985	2,155
1857-O	2,040	2,950
1857-S	1,965	2,155
1858	2,040	2,145

	VF	XF
1858-O	2,250	3,850
1858-S	1,965	2,175
1859	2,040	2,450
1859-O	6,400	16,500
1859-S	1,965	2,155
1860	1,965	2,155
1860-O	3,650	14,500
1860-S	1,985	2,445
1861	1,965	2,155
1861-O	5,650	17,500

	VF	XF
1861-S	1,985	2,255
1862	1,965	3,500
1862-S	1,950	2,030
1863	1,965	2,650
1863-S	1,950	2,110
1864	1,965	2,045
1864-S	1,950	2,090
1865	1,965	2,110
1865-S	1,950	2,110
1866-S	2,750	11,500

Motto above eagle

A congressional act passed March 3, 1865, allowed the addition of the motto "In God We Trust" to all U.S. gold and silver coins.

	VF	XF
1866	1,910	2,075
1866-S	1,910	2,085
1867	1,910	2,100
1867-S	1,910	2,085
1868	1,950	2,185
1866-S	1,910	2,055
1869	1,920	2,045

	VF	XF
1869-S	1,910	2,075
1870	1,930	2,075
1870-CC	200,000	275,000
1870-S	1,910	2,030
1871	1,920	2,030
1871-CC	9,500	19,500
1871-S	1,910	2,045

	VF	XF
1872	1,910	2,075
1872-CC	2,550	5,450
1872-S	1,910	2,075
1873 closed 3	1,910	2,135
1873 open 3	1,910	2,075
1873-CC	2,900	4,750
1873-S closed 3	1,910	2,045
1873-S open 3	1,910	2,075

	VF	XF
1874	1,910	2,075
1874-CC	2,100	2,450
1874-S	1,910	2,045
1875	1,910	2,075
1875-CC	1,950	2,250
1875-S	1,910	2,045
1876	1,910	2,065
1876-CC	1,960	2,300
1876-S	1,910	2,045

"Twenty Dollars" on reverse

The reverse design was modified so the denomination read "Twenty Dollars" instead of "Twenty D."

	VF	XF
1877	1,830	1,970
1877-CC	1,985	2,150
1877-S	1,820	1,870
1878	1,840	1,970
1878-CC	2,450	3,950
1878-S	1,820	1,845
1879	1,900	1,970
1879-CC	3,000	4,850
1879-O	12,500	21,500

	VF	XF
1879-S	1,820	1,845
1880	1,930	2,000
1880-S	1,820	1,845
1881	12,500	21,000
1881-S	1,820	1,845
1882	13,500	39,500
1882-CC	1,970	2,000
1882-S	1,820	1,845
1883		proof 27,500

	VF	XF
1883-CC	1,970	2,000
1883-S	1,820	1,845
1884		*proof* 35,000
1884-CC	1,970	2,000
1884-S	1,820	1,845
1885	8,450	13,850
1885-CC	2,500	3,850
1885-S	1,820	1,845
1886	10,500	18,500
1887		*AU* 26,500
1887-S	1,820	1,845
1888	1,820	1,845
1888-S	1,820	1,845
1889	1,980	2,100
1889-CC	1,970	2,150
1889-S	1,820	1,845
1890	1,820	1,870
1890-CC	1,970	2,000
1890-S	1,820	1,845
1891	8,500	15,000
1891-CC	4,950	9,000
1891-S	1,820	1,845
1892	2,000	3,650
1892-CC	1,970	2,100
1892-S	1,820	1,845
1893	1,820	1,865
1893-CC	2,070	2,100
1893-S	1,780	1,800
1894	1,780	1,800

	VF	XF
1894-S	1,780	1,800
1895	1,780	1,800
1895-S	1,780	1,800
1896	1,780	1,800
1896-S	1,780	1,800
1897	1,780	1,800
1897-S	1,780	1,800
1898	1,785	1,830
1898-S	1,785	1,800
1899	1,780	1,800
1899-S	1,780	1,800
1900	1,780	1,800
1900-S	1,780	1,800
1901	1,780	1,800
1901-S	1,780	1,800
1902	1,780	2,000
1902-S	1,780	1,800
1903	1,780	1,800
1903-S	1,780	1,800
1904	1,780	1,800
1904-S	1,780	1,800
1905	1,785	1,820
1905-S	1,780	1,800
1906	1,785	1,800
1906-D	1,780	1,800
1906-S	1,780	1,800
1907	1,780	1,800
1907-D	1,780	1,800
1907-S	1,780	1,800

SAINT-GAUDENS

Sculptor Augustus Saint-Gaudens designed President Theodore Roosevelt's inaugural medal. Roosevelt liked the result so much that he commissioned the sculptor to improve the design of U.S. coinage. The results included a striking new design for the gold $20 coin in 1907, considered by many to be the most beautiful coin in U.S. history. Roosevelt wanted the new $20 coin to emulate the high-relief style of ancient Greek coins.

Date in Roman numerals

Size: *34 millimeters.* **Weight:** *33.436 grams.*
Composition: *90 percent gold (0.9677 troy ounces), 10 percent copper.*

	VF	XF
MCMVII (1907) wire rim	7,650	8,750

	VF	XF
MCMVII (1907) flat rim	7,900	9,250

Date in Arabic numerals

Although an artistic triumph, the high relief of the first 1907 Saint-Gaudens gold $20 coins caused production problems and would not allow the coins to stack properly. Thus, the relief was lowered, and Arabic numerals were used in the date instead of Roman numerals.

	VF	XF
1907	1,795	1,825
1908	1,785	1,820

	VF	XF
1908-D	1,795	1,830

Motto below eagle

Congressional acts of March 3, 1865, and Feb. 12, 1873, allowed the motto "In God We Trust" to be placed on U.S. coins but did not mandate it. According to author Don Taxay, President Theodore Roosevelt considered it sacrilege to use a religious motto on coinage. When the new 1907 gold $10 and $20 appeared without the motto, Congress passed legislation on May 18, 1908, mandating its use on all coins on which it had previously appeared.

The Gold Reserve Act of Jan. 30, 1934, discontinued the production of all U.S. gold coinage. Most of the 1933 gold $20 coins produced were still in government vaults at the time and were melted, but a few examples illicitly found their way into private hands. The U.S. government allowed one of them to be sold in 2002, but any others that turn up are still subject to confiscation.

	VF	XF
1908	1,790	1,825
1908-D	1,795	1,830
1908-S	2,450	3,150
1909	1,800	1,850
1909-D	1,835	1,870
1909-S	1,795	1,830
1910	1,790	1,825
1910-D	1,790	1,825
1910-S	1,795	1,830
1911	1,795	1,830

	VF	XF
1911-D	1,790	1,825
1911-S	1,790	1,825
1912	1,795	1,830
1913	1,795	1,830
1913-D	1,790	1,825
1913-S	1,845	1,880
1914	1,800	1,840
1914-D	1,790	1,825
1914-S	1,790	1,825
1915	1,795	1,830

	VF	XF
1915-S	1,790	1,825
1916-S	1,795	1,830
1920	1,785	1,820
1920-S	14,500	18,500
1921	35,000	43,500
1922	1,785	1,820
1922-S	1,900	2,000
1923	1,785	1,820
1923-D	1,795	1,830
1924	1,785	1,820
1924-D	2,010	2,040
1924-S	1,665	1,750
1925	1,785	1,820
1925-D	1,950	2,100

	VF	XF
1925-S	1,900	2,850
1926	1,785	1,820
1926-D	10,000	15,500
1926-S	1,490	1,550
1927	1,785	1,820
1927-D	155,000	200,000
1927-S	6,850	8,850
1928	1,785	1,820
1929	10,000	13,500
1930-S	35,000	41,000
1931	10,500	13,500
1931-D	8,850	11,500
1932	12,500	14,500
1933 *13 known*		

2009 ultrahigh relief

Size: *27 millimeters.* **Weight:** *31.1 grams.* **Composition:** *99.99 percent gold (1 troy ounce).* **Notes:** *The 2009 ultrahigh-relief gold $20 revived the classic Saint-Gaudens gold $20 design for one year only in a special issue sold by the U.S. Mint at a premium directly to collectors.*

	PF-65
2009	3,300

Paper money introduction

The first paper money to circulate in the United States was issued during the Colonial era. British mercantile policies resulted in a chronic shortage of precious metal coinage in the Colonies, and the paper issues helped fill the void.

During the Revolutionary War, the states and Continental Congress continued to issue paper money, but its backing in hard currency was spotty at best. Inflation ensued, and the notes' value plummeted. Some were called "shinplasters" because early Americans put them in their boots to help keep their feet warm. The saying "not worth a Continental" had its roots in the devaluation of Continental currency.

Designs on state notes varied, but most featured inscriptions within elaborate borders. Coats of arms and crowns were also common. During the mid-1770s, designs became more elaborate; farm scenes and buildings were popular design subjects. Most Continental currency bore intricate circular seals of allegories.

To deter counterfeiting, leaves were used in the printing process. The fine detail of a leaf on a note was difficult for counterfeiters to duplicate. Each note was hand signed, sometimes by important figures in early American history. The significance of a note's signatures can enhance its value.

Because of the devaluation of paper money during the Colonial and Continental Congress eras, the Constitution specified that "no state shall … make anything but gold and silver coin a tender in payment of debts." This provision, however, still allowed banks and other private institutions to issue paper money, which circulated solely on the people's trust in the issuing entity. Sound banks kept enough hard money reserves to redeem their notes on demand; less scrupulous banks didn't.

Known as "obsolete notes" or "broken bank notes" today, these private issues were produced in especially large numbers in the 1830s and 1850s. They became obsolete in the 1860s when many of the issuing banks went under while others redeemed their outstanding notes and did not issue more. The notes are valued by collectors today because many of them feature artistic vignettes of local industries, such as shipping or cotton, or patriotic themes provided by the printer. Some show their value in coins – two half dollars and a quarter to represent $1.25, for example. Most obsolete notes are one-sided.

During the Civil War, the public hoarded gold, silver, and even copper coins. In response to the resulting coin shortage, postage stamps were used for small change in everyday transactions. The stamps were placed in small envelopes printed with a value, but the envelopes deteriorated quickly and the stamps soon became a sticky mess.

The solution was to issue small, rectangular-shaped "postage currency" in 1862. Depictions of postage stamps on the currency indicated their value; a 50-cent note depicted 50 cents in postage stamps, for example. They could not be used as postage on letters or packages (they had no adhesive), but they could be redeemed at any post office for the indicated amount of postage.

In 1863, fractional currency replaced the postage currency. It was similar in size to the postage currency but did not contain any reference to postage stamps. Fractional notes were issued through 1876, by which time coinage production had caught up with demand and the hoarding of the Civil War era had ended. Fractional currency is common in the collectibles market today. Many issues can be purchased for $20 to $100, depending on the individual note and its condition.

Demand notes are considered the first regular paper money issued by the U.S. government and lead off the listings that follow.

The paper money issues in the following listings are identified first by type, using the names commonly used by collectors. They are further identified by denomination and series date, which is not necessarily the date in which the piece was issued. "Series" indicates the year of the act authorizing the series or the year production of the series began. Further means of identifying notes include their design, seal color, issuing bank, signers, and size. Through 1928, U.S. paper money issues were about 7 1/2 inches by 3 1/8 inches and are commonly called "large-size notes" today. Beginning with Series 1928 (released in 1929), U.S. paper money issues were reduced to 6 1/8 inches by 2 5/8 inches and are commonly called "small-size notes."

GRADING U.S. PAPER MONEY

Crisp uncirculated (CU) describes a perfectly preserved note that never has been mishandled by the issuing authority, a bank teller, the public, or a collector. The paper is clean and firm without discoloration. Corners are sharp and square, with no evidence of rounding. (Rounded corners often indicate a cleaned or "doctored" note.) The note will have its original, natural sheen.

About uncirculated (AU) describes a virtually perfect note that shows signs of some minor handling. It may show evidence of bank-counting folds at a corner or one light fold through the center but not both. An AU note cannot be creased (a crease is defined as a hard fold that has usually broken the note's surface). The paper is clean and bright with original sheen. Corners are not rounded.

Extremely fine (XF) describes an attractive note with signs of light handling. It may have a maximum of three light folds or one strong crease. The paper is clean and bright with original sheen. Corners may show only the slightest evidence of rounding. There may also be the slightest signs of wear where a fold meets the edge.

Very fine (VF) describes an attractive note with more evidence of handling and wear. Vertical and horizontal folds may be present. The paper may have minimal dirt or color smudging. The paper itself is still relatively crisp and not floppy. There should be no tears in the border area, although the edges will show slight wear. Corners will also show wear but not full rounding.

Fine (F) describes a note that has seen considerable circulation. Many folds, creases, and wrinkling will be present. The paper is not excessively dirty but may have some softness. Edges may show signs of much handling with minor tears in the border area. Tears may not extend into the design. There should be no center hole from excessive folding. Colors should be clear, but they may not be very bright. A staple hole or two is not considered unusual wear on a note grading fine. The note's overall appearance is still desirable.

Very good (VG) describes a well-used but still intact note. Corners may have much wear and rounding. There may be tiny nicks, tears extending into the design, some discoloration and staining, and possibly a small center hole from excessive folding. Staple and pin holes are usually present, and the paper itself is quite limp.

Good (G) describes a well-worn and heavily used note. Normal damage from prolonged circulation may include strong multiple folds and creases, stains, staple or pin holes or both, dirt, discoloration, edge tears, a center hole, rounded corners, and an overall unattractive appearance. No large pieces of the note may be missing.

Fair (F) describes a totally limp, dirty, and well-used note. Large pieces may be torn off or missing.

Poor (P) describes a note with severe damage from wear, staining, missing pieces, graffiti, and larger holes. Tape may be holding pieces of the note together. Rough edges may have been trimmed off.

In addition, follow these rules for handling collectible paper money:

Folding always damages a note. Never fold a piece of collectible paper money.

Cleaning, washing, and pressing paper money is also harmful and reduces a note's grade and subsequent value. A washed or pressed note will probably lose its original sheen, and its surface may become lifeless and dull. A pressed note may still show evidence of folds and creases under a good light, and washed notes may have white streaks where the folds or creases were.

Demand notes

The demand notes of 1861 were the first paper money issued by the U.S. government, as an emergency measure during the Civil War. At first, they were not officially legal tender, so merchants and other private individuals were not obligated to accept them in payment for goods and services. But they were "receivable in payment for all public dues," so they could be used to pay taxes, for example. Later, a law was passed requiring their acceptance in private transactions also. The name "demand notes" comes from the statement on their face: "The United States promises to pay to the bearer on demand."

There were limits, however, on how demand notes could be redeemed. The notes were issued at five cities and could be redeemed by the assistant treasurers only in the individual note's specific city of issue.

Designs were uniform among issues from all cities. The $5 note shows at left the statue of Columbia from the U.S. Capitol and at right a portrait of Alexander Hamilton. The $10 shows Abraham Lincoln (then in office) at left, an eagle in the center, and an allegorical figure of art at right. The $20 depicts Liberty holding a sword and shield. The nickname "greenback" for paper money began with these notes, which have a distinctive green back. The privately issued obsolete notes, which preceded demand notes, had blank backs.

There are two major varieties of demand notes. Originally clerks were to hand sign the notes as "for the" Treasury register and "for the" U.S. treasurer. To save clerks the time required to write "for the" millions of times, the words were printed on later notes instead of handwritten. The earlier variety, with "for the" handwritten, are worth more than the prices listed here.

High-grade notes in this series are rare.

	F	VF
$5 Boston	3,200	5,500
$5 Cincinnati *rare*		
$5 New York	3,400	4,400
$5 Philadelphia	3,300	4,500
$5 St. Louis	18,000	38,000

	F	VF
$10 Boston	18,000	22,000
$10 Cincinnati	16,000	20,000
$10 New York	10,000	20,000
$10 Philadelphia	5,000	15,000
$10 St. Louis	12,000	75,000

	F	VF
$20 Boston	—	75,000
$20 Cincinnati	2,500	—
$20 New York	—	80,500
$20 Philadelphia	—	100,000

Treasury notes

Treasury notes are also called "coin notes" because the Treasury secretary was required to redeem them in his choice of gold or silver coin, although the notes were backed by silver bullion rather than coins.

Treasury notes were issued only in 1890 and 1891. Both years have the same face designs, generally of military heroes. The original reverse designs featured the values spelled out in large letters. For 1891, they were redesigned to allow more blank space. The ornamentation of the two 0s in 100 on the reverse of the $100 notes looks like the pattern on the skin of a watermelon. Hence, they are known in the collecting community as "watermelon notes."

	F	XF
$1 1890 Edwin M. Stanton	400	2,000
$1 1891 Edwin M. Stanton	210	450

	F	XF
$2 1890 Gen. James D. McPherson	650	4,000
$2 1891 Gen. James D. McPherson	460	1,400

	F	XF
$5 1890 Gen. George H. Thomas	550	5,800

	F	XF

$5 1891 Gen. George H. Thomas 550 1,400

	F	XF

$10 1890 Gen. Philip H. Sheridan 1,400 5,500
$10 1891 Gen. Philip H. Sheridan 1,000 2,500

	F	XF
$20 1890 John Marshall	3,125	10,000

	F	XF
$20 1891 John Marshall	8,500	17,500

F	XF

$50 1891 William H. Seward ....— 125,000

V	XF

$100 1890 Adm. David G. Farragut ....— 185,000

	F	XF

$100 1891 Adm. David G. Farragut 63,250 150,000
$1,000 1890 Gen. George Meade .... — ...1,095,000

	F	XF

$1,000 1891 Gen. George Meade *rare* ....

National bank notes

National bank notes were a collaboration between private, nationally charted banks and the U.S. government. Individual banks could invest in U.S. bonds and, in return, receive paper money with a face value equal to their investment. The federal government designed and printed the notes. Designs were the same for each bank, but notes were imprinted with the name and charter number of the national bank receiving them. Some early notes also bear the coat of arms of the issuing bank's state.

National bank notes, titled "National Currency" on their faces, were legal tender anywhere in the United States and could be redeemed at the issuing bank or the U.S. Treasury. Notes redeemed at the Treasury were charged against the issuing bank's bond account. More than 1,300 national banks issued notes.

There were three periods during which banks could apply for a 20-year nationally issued charter: (1) 1863-1882, (2) 1882-1902, and (3) 1902-1922. Banks could issue notes under the first charter period until 1902, under the second charter period until 1922, and under the third charter period until 1929. Notes issued under each charter period have different designs.

Like all other U.S. paper money, national bank notes were reduced in size in 1929. Type 1 notes (1929-1933) list the charter number on the face twice. Type 2 notes (1933-1935) list it four times.

National bank notes were discontinued in May 1935 when the Treasury recalled many of the bonds in which the national banks had invested.

Nationals have been among the most sought-after notes in a generally active U.S. paper money market. Not all nationals of a given type have the same value; notes of certain states and cities are more popularly collected than others. Also, some banks ordered only small quantities of notes. The values listed below are for the most common and least expensive banks issuing that type of note. Large-size nationals from Alaska, Arizona, Hawaii, Idaho, Indian Territory, Mississippi, Nevada, New Mexico, Puerto Rico, and South Dakota are worth more. The same is true for small-size nationals from Alaska, Arizona, Hawaii, Idaho, Montana, Nevada, and Wyoming.

FIRST CHARTER (1863-1875)

	VG	VF
$1 Allegory of Concord, no date, original series	600	1,050
$1 Allegory of Concord, 1875	600	1,050
$2 Sir Walter Raleigh, "lazy 2," no date, original series	3,600	5,750

	VG	VF
$2 Sir Walter Raleigh, 1875	1,500	4,000

	VG	VF
$5 Columbus sighting land, no date, original series	725	1,650
$5 Columbus sighting land, 1875	725	1,650

	VG	VF
$10 Franklin flying kite, no date, original series	1,000	2,000
$10 Franklin flying kite, 1875	1,000	2,000
$20 Battle of Lexington, no date, original series	2,500	4,000

	VG	VF
$20 Battle of Lexington, 1875	1,600	3,250
$50 Washington crossing the Delaware, no date, original series	15,000	25,000

	VG	VF
$50 Washington crossing the Delaware, 1875	15,000	25,000
$100 Battle of Lake Erie, no date, original series	17,000	35,000
$100 Battle of Lake Erie, 1875	17,000	35,000
$500 Arrival of the Sirius, no date, original series *rare*		
$500 Arrival of the Sirius, 1875 *rare*		
$1,000 Scott entering Mexico City, no date, original series *rare*		
$1,000 Scott entering Mexico City, 1875 *1 known*		

SECOND CHARTER, SERIES OF 1882, "BROWN BACKS," CHARTER NUMBER ON BACK

	VG	VF
$5 James Garfield	450	650

	VG	VF
$10 Franklin flying kite	500	750
$20 Battle of Lexington	575	850
$50 Washington crossing the Delaware	4,500	5,175

	VG	VF
$100 Battle of Lake Erie	5,500	10,350

SECOND CHARTER, SERIES OF 1882,
"DATE BACKS," LARGE "1882*1908" ON BACK

	VG	VF
$5 James Garfield	425	575

	VG	VF
$10 Franklin flying kite	400	800

	VG	VF
$20 Battle of Lexington	550	800

	VG	VF

$50 Washington crossing the Delaware...................................5,500 6,500

	VG	VF

$100 Battle of Lake Erie.. 7,500 8,250

SECOND CHARTER, SERIES OF 1882, "VALUE BACKS," VALUE SPELLED OUT ON BACK

	VG	VF
$5 James Garfield	500	1,025
$10 Franklin flying kite	450	800
$20 Battle of Lexington	750	1,300
$50 Washington crossing the Delaware, *rare*		
$100 Battle of Lake Erie *rare*		

THIRD CHARTER, SERIES OF 1902, RED TREASURY SEAL ON FACE

	VG	VF
$5 Benjamin Harrison	400	550

	VG	VF
$10 William McKinley	350	850
$20 Hugh McCulloch	450	625

	VG	VF
$50 John Sherman	5,750	6,000

	VG	VF
$100 John Knox	7,500	11,000

THIRD CHARTER, SERIES OF 1902, BLUE TREASURY SEAL, "1902-1908" ON BACK

	VG	VF
$5 Benjamin Harrison	150	350
$10 William McKinley	150	350

	VG	VF
$20 Hugh McCulloch	175	325 ✓
$50 John Sherman	700	825

	VG	VF
$100 John Knox	850	1,250

THIRD CHARTER, SERIES OF 1902, BLUE TREASURY SEAL, "PLAIN BACKS," WITHOUT DATES

	VG	VF
$5 Benjamin Harrison	100	200

	VG	VF
$10 William McKinley	125	225
$20 Hugh McCulloch	150	300
$50 John Sherman	700	825
$100 John Knox	800	1,250

THIRD CHARTER, SERIES OF 1929, BROWN TREASURY SEAL, SMALL SIZE

	VG	VF
$5 Type 1	50.00	100
$5 Type 2	60.00	100

	VG	VF
$10 Type 1	60.00	90
$10 Type 2	75.00	175

	VG	VF
$20 Type 1	60.00	85.00
$20 Type 2	70.00	125
$50 Type 1	80.00	125
$50 Type 2	200	400

	VG	VF
$100 Type 1	175	250
$100 Type 2	225	350

National gold bank notes

National gold bank notes were similar to national bank notes but were redeemable specifically in gold coin. They were issued by nationally chartered banks that were authorized by the Treasury to issue notes redeemable in gold.

They were issued from 1870 to 1875 to relieve California banks from handling mass quantities of gold coin. All but one of the banks authorized to issue the notes were located in California.

National gold bank notes were printed on golden-yellow paper and depict an assortment of U.S. gold coins on their reverse designs. Fine engraving resulted in high-quality images.

Because other types of notes were not popular in California, national gold bank notes saw heavy use and are scarce today in collectible condition.

	G	F
$5 Columbus sighting land	1,750	7,500

	G	F

$10 Franklin flying kite 4,000 20,000

	G	F

$20 Battle of Lexington 8,000 30,000

	G	F

$50 Washington crossing the Delaware *rare*..

	G	F

$100 Battle of Lake Erie...100,000 258,000

United States notes

Most of these notes are titled "United States Note" at the top or bottom of their faces, but some earlier ones are titled "Treasury Note." The first United States notes omit both, but all were authorized under the same legislation. They were issued for more than a century (1862-1966) and thus are the longest-running type of U.S. paper money.

The series contains many classic designs. The most popular is the $10 with a bison on its face.

Like other currency, United States notes were reduced in size with Series 1928, printed in 1929. Small-size United States notes occasionally are still found in circulation today and are distinguished by a red Treasury seal. They generally are not collectible in worn condition.

This series includes popular "star notes," which have part of the serial number replaced by a star. They were printed to replace notes accidentally destroyed in manufacturing. These were introduced on $20 notes in 1880 and eventually descended to $1 notes by 1917. They usually are worth more than regularly numbered notes.

LARGE SIZE

	F	XF
$1 1862 Salmon P. Chase, red seal	325	850

	F	XF
$1 1869 George Washington	400	2,200
$1 1874 George Washington	200	835
$1 1875 George Washington	200	600
$1 1878 George Washington	275	650
$1 1880 George Washington	200	400
$1 1917 George Washington	60	115

	F	XF
$1 1923 George Washington	125	275

	F	XF

$2 1862 Alexander Hamilton 650 2,300

	F	XF

$2 1869 Jefferson, Capitol... 700 3,250
$2 1874 Jefferson, Capitol... 460 1,200
$2 1875 Jefferson, Capitol... 480 1,200
$2 1878 Jefferson, Capitol... 380 800
$2 1880 Jefferson, Capitol...275 600

	F	XF

$5 1862 Statue of Columbia, Alexander Hamilton 575 1,750
$5 1863 same, different obligation on back 450 1,100

	F	XF

$5 1869 Andrew Jackson, pioneer family 600 1,800
$5 1875 same, red seal 250 700
$5 1880 same, brown seal 440 600

	F	XF
$10 1862 Lincoln, allegory of art	1,000	2,250
$10 1863 same, different obligation on back	1,450	3,000

	F	XF
$10 1869 Daniel Webster, Pocahontas	1,300	1,800
$10 1875 same, different obligation on back	1,000	3,000
$10 1878 same	1,150	2,250
$10 1880 same, brown seal	500	1,300
$10 1880 same, large red seal	400	1,000
$10 1880 same, small red seal	375	1,250

	F	XF

$10 1901 bison...600 2,000

	F	XF

$10 1923 Andrew Jackson.. 1,750 5,250

	F	XF

$20 1862 Liberty with sword and shield 2,300 6,750
$20 1863 same, different obligation on back.........................2,000 4,000

	F	XF
$20 1869 Alexander Hamilton, Victory	2,900	10,000
$20 1875 same, no inscription at center on back	1,500	2,750
$20 1878 same	900	1,800
$20 1880 same, brown seal	750	2,500
$20 1880 same, large red seal	400	1,750
$20 1880 same, small red seal	350	1,250

	F	XF
$50 1862 Alexander Hamilton	32,500	43,125
$50 1863 same, different obligation on back	12,500	300,000

	F	XF
$50 1869 Peace, Henry Clay	21,500	50,000

	F	XF
$50 1874 Benjamin Franklin, Columbia	10,000	15,000
$50 1875 same, *rare*		
$50 1878 same	5,000	20,000
$50 1880 same, brown seal	5,000	30,000
$50 1880 same, large red seal	6,000	14,000
$50 1880 same, small red seal	2,000	6,325

	F	XF
$100 1862 eagle	30,000	50,000
$100 1863 same, different obligation on back, *rare*		

	F	XF
$100 1869 Lincoln, allegory of Architecture	17,500	18,400
$100 1875 same	15,000	40,000
$100 1878 same	15,000	30,000
$100 1880 same, inscription at left on back, brown seal	9,000	30,000
$100 1880 same, large red seal	14,000	35,000
$100 1880 same, small red seal	6,000	17,500
$500 1862 Albert Gallatin, *rare*		
$500 1863 same, different obligation on back, *rare*		
$500 1869 John Quincy Adams, *rare*		
$500 1874 Gen. Joseph Mansfield, *rare*		
$500 1875 same, *rare*		
$500 1878 same, *rare*		

	F	XF

$500 1880 Gen. Joseph Mansfield, brown seal, *rare*..

$500 1880 same, large red seal, *rare* ....

$500 1880 same, small red seal, *rare* ....

$1,000 1862 Robert Morris, *none known*...

$1,000 1863 same, different obligation on back, *rare* ....

$1,000 1869 Columbus, DeWitt Clinton, *rare*..

$1,000 1878 same, *rare*...

$1,000 1880 same, inscription at left, brown seal *rare*...

$1,000 1880 same, large red seal, *rare* ....

$1,000 1880 same, small red seal, *rare*...

SMALL SIZE, RED SEAL

Denomination	Series	Front	Back
$1	1928	Washington	ONE
$2	1928-1963A	Jefferson	Monticello
$5	1928-1963	Lincoln	Lincoln Memorial
$100	1966-1966A	Franklin	Independence Hall

	F	XF

$1 1928 ....125 225

	F	XF

$2 1928A ....20.00 .... 75.00
$2 1928B 75.00 300
$2 1928C ....20.00 ....65.00
$2 1928D ....20.00 ....45.00
$2 1928E ....30.00 ....50.00
$2 1928F .... 15.00 ....25.00
$2 1928G ....10.00 ....25.00
$2 1953 ....10.00 .... 15.00
$2 1953A .... 8.00 .... 12.00
$2 1953B ....7.00 .... 10.00
$2 1953C ....7.00 .... 10.00
$2 1963 ....7.00 .... 15.00
$2 1963A ....7.00 ....9.00

	F	XF
$5 1928	15.00	35.00
$5 1928A	20.00	50.00
$5 1928B	15.00	30.00
$5 1928C	13.00	30.00
$5 1928D	40.00	75.00
$5 1928E	15.00	25.00
$5 1928F	10.00	50.00
$5 1953	10.00	15.00
$5 1953A	10.00	18.00
$5 1953B	10.00	15.00
$5 1953C	10.00	25.00
$5 1963	8.00	15.00

	F	XF
$100 1966	125	240
$100 1966A	150	200

Gold certificates

As the title on these notes implies, gold certificates were backed by reserves of gold coin and payable to the bearer in gold coin. The first gold certificates were issued from 1865 to 1875 but were used only for transactions between banks. Notes of this period not listed here are not known to have survived. The issue of 1882 was the first for general circulation. Only $5,000 and $10,000 notes were issued in 1888-1889 and did not circulate widely.

Regular issues were again placed in circulation from 1905 to 1907. Gold certificates of Series 1913-1928 are the most common. Gold certificates were reduced in size beginning with Series 1928. The small-size notes have a gold Treasury seal.

The final gold certificates, of 1934, were again issued just for bank transactions. The government recalled these notes from general circulation in 1933 when it withdrew gold coinage. Today, they are legal to own but are scarce because of the recall.

LARGE SIZE

F	XF

FIRST ISSUE, 1863

$20 eagle on shield ....— 500,000

 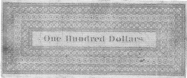

F	XF

$100 eagle on shield, *rare* ....

SECOND ISSUE, 1870-1871

None known ....

THIRD ISSUE, 1875

$100 Thomas H. Benton, *rare*...

FOURTH ISSUE, SERIES OF 1882

	F	XF
$20 James Garfield, brown seal	2,500	7,500
$20 same, red seal	575	2,800
$50 Silas Wright	1,550	5,000
$100 Thomas Benton, brown seal, rare		
$100 same, large red seal, rare		
$100 same, small red seal	1,150	3,500
$500 Abraham Lincoln	10,500	25,000

	F	XF
$1,000 Alexander Hamilton, brown seal, *1 known*		
$1,000 same, large red seal, *1 known*		
$1,000 same, small red seal	—	230,000
$5,000 James Madison, *rare*		
$10,000 Andrew Jackson, *rare*		

FIFTH ISSUE, SERIES OF 1888

	F	XF
$10,000 Andrew Jackson, *rare*		

SIXTH ISSUE, SERIES OF 1900

	F	XF
$10,000 Andrew Jackson	1,750	3,750

SEVENTH ISSUE, SERIES OF 1905-1907

	F	XF
$10 1907 Michael Hillegas	175	500

	F	XF
$20 1905 George Washington	1,000	15,000
$20 1906 George Washington	200	650

EIGHTH ISSUE, SERIES OF 1907

	F	XF
$1,000 Alexander Hamilton	15,000	37,500

NINTH ISSUE, SERIES OF 1913

	F	XF
$50 Ulysses S. Grant	450	3,450

TENTH ISSUE, SERIES OF 1922

	F	XF
$10 Michael Hillegas	140	800
$20 George Washington	200	525
$50 Ulysses S. Grant	425	1,625

	F	XF

$100 Thomas Benton 700 3,000

	F	XF

$500 Abraham Lincoln .... — 50,000
$1,000 Alexander Hamilton .... — 80,500

SMALL SIZE

SERIES OF 1928

	VF	XF

$10 Alexander Hamilton 145 200

	VF	XF

$20 Andrew Jackson 155 250

	VF	XF

$50 Ulysses S. Grant 600 900

	VF	XF

$100 Benjamin Franklin 650 1,750

	VF	XF

$500 William McKinley...9,000 15,000

	VF	XF

$1,000 Grover Cleveland 8,000 15,000
$5,000 James Madison *1 known* ....

Silver certificates

On Feb. 28, 1878, the same day Congress authorized the striking of millions of silver dollars, it also passed legislation authorizing silver certificates. The notes represented actual silver dollars held by the U.S. Treasury. The legislation passed in response to lobbying by silver-mining interests.

Some of the most famous and beautiful bank notes issued by the United States are silver certificates. These include the "educational" $1, $2, and $5 notes of 1896; the "One Papa" $5; and the "porthole" $5. "One Papa" is a misnomer. The note actually depicts Chief Running Antelope of the Uncpapa Sioux, but because the name was unfamiliar to early collectors, it was mispronounced "Chief One Papa."

Like other U.S. paper money, silver certificates were reduced in size with Series 1928, in 1929.

During World War II, there was fear that supplies of U.S. currency would fall into enemy hands if certain territories were lost. In response, notes distributed in these territories were given distinguishing features that permitted their identification and repudiation if captured. Silver certificates issued to troops in North Africa were printed with a yellow Treasury seal instead of a blue one. Notes distributed in Hawaii featured the word "Hawaii" overprinted in large letters on the back.

The motto "In God We Trust" was added to the $1 note for Series 1935G and 1935H, and all 1957 series. Silver certificates continued until Series 1957B, in 1963. Small-size silver certificates are occasionally found in circulation today and are easily recognized by their blue Treasury seal. When worn, these notes are generally not collectible but do have some novelty value. They have not been redeemable for silver dollars since 1968.

This series includes popular "star notes," which have part of the serial number replaced by a star. They were printed to replace notes accidentally destroyed in the manufacturing process. Star notes were introduced in 1899. They often, but not always, are worth somewhat more than regularly numbered pieces.

LARGE SIZE

	F	XF

$1 1886 Martha Washington, small red seal 250 500
$1 1886 same, large red seal 300 550
$1 1886 same, brown seal 250 700
$1 1891 Martha Washington 275 800

	F	XF

$1 1896 History instructing youth 350 800

	F	XF

$1 1899 eagle 150 225

	F	XF

$1 1923 George Washington ....35.00 ....60.00

| | F | XF |

$2 1886 Gen. Winfield Scott Hancock, small red seal.............600 1,500
$2 1886 same, large red seal...500 1,500
$2 1886 same, brown seal...500 2,100

| | F | XF |

$2 1891 William Windom 475 1,800

| | F | XF |

$2 1896 Science presenting steam and electricity
to Commerce and Industry 625 2,550

| | F | XF |

$2 1899 George Washington, Mechanics and Agriculture... 200 500

	F	XF

$5 1886 Ulysses S. Grant, small red seal 1,250 5,000
$5 1886 same, large red seal.. 1,000 4,500
$5 1886 same, brown seal.. 1,300 4,250
$5 1891 Ulysses S. Grant 500 1,500

	F	XF

$5 1896 winged Electricity lighting the world 650 4,500

	F	XF

$5 1899 Chief Running Antelope 450 1,200

	F	XF

$5 1923 Abraham Lincoln 650 2,300

	F	XF
$10 1878 Robert Morris	—	40,000
$10 1880 same, brown seal	1,700	8,500
$10 1880 same, red seal	3,500	20,000

	F	XF
$10 1886 Thomas Hendricks, small red seal	1,250	5,000
$10 1886 same, large red seal	1,250	4,000
$10 1886 same, brown seal	1,000	5,000
$10 1891 Thomas Hendricks	600	2,000

	F	XF
$20 1878 Capt. Stephen Decatur	5,000	25,000
$20 1880 same	7,500	20,000
$20 1880 same, brown seal	3,000	11,000
$20 1880 same, red seal	6,000	22,000

	F	XF
$20 1886 Daniel Manning, small red seal	—	35,000
$20 1886 same, large red seal	5,000	50,000
$20 1886 same, brown seal	3,000	16,000
$20 1891 same, red seal	1,000	3,750
$20 1891 same, blue seal	700	3,450

	F	XF
$50 1878 Edward Everett		CU 37,000
$50 1880 same, brown seal	10,000	35,000
$50 1880 same, red seal	27,500	52,500
$50 1891 same, red seal	2,500	7,000
$50 1891 same, blue seal	1,500	6,600

	F	XF
$100 1878 James Monroe, *rare*		
$100 1880 same, brown seal	16,000	45,000
$100 1800 same, red seal	—	125,000
$100 1891 same	8,000	43,125
$500 1878 Charles Sumner, *rare*		
$500 1880 same	—	420,000
$1,000 1878, William Marcy, *none known*		
$1,000 1880 William Marcy	—	580,000
$1,000 1891 Liberty, Marcy *rare*		

SMALL SIZE, BLUE SEAL

Denomination	Series	Front	Back
$1	1928-1928E	Washington	ONE
$1	1934-1957B	Washington	Great Seal
$5	1934-1953C	Lincoln	Lincoln Memorial
$10	1933-1953B	Hamilton	Treasury building

	F	XF
$1 1928	25.00	50.00
$1 1928A	25.00	45.00
$1 1928B	25.00	45.00
$1 1928C	125	450
$1 1928D	60.00	200
$1 1928E	400	1,100
$1 1934	25.00	40.00
$1 1935	10.00	15.00
$1 1935A	3.00	6.00

	F	XF
$1 1935A "Hawaii"	45.00	70.00

	F	XF

$1 1935A yellow seal ....45.00 .... 95.00

	F	XF

$1 1935A red R..75.00 130

	F	XF

$1 1935A red S...75.00 150
$1 1935B.. 3.00 .... 5.00
$1 1935C.. 2.00 .... 4.00
$1 1935D.. 3.00 .... 6.00
$1 1935E.. 3.00 .... 4.00
$1 1935F.. 3.00 .... 4.00
$1 1935G.. 3.00 .... 5.00
$1 1935G "In God We Trust" .... 3.00 .... 10.00
$1 1935H.. 3.00 .... 5.00
$1 1957 .... 3.00 .... 4.00
$1 1957A.. 3.00 .... 4.00
$1 1957B.. 3.00 .... 4.00
$5 1934..15.00 .... 40.00

	F	XF
$5 1934 "Hawaii"	75.00	200
$5 1934A	15.00	30.00

	F	XF
$5 1934A yellow seal	70.00	100
$5 1934B	10.00	25.00
$5 1934C	10.00	30.00
$5 1934D	10.00	20.00
$5 1953	10.00	25.00
$5 1953A	8.00	15.00
$5 1953B	8.00	15.00

	F	XF
$10 1933	3,500	7,000
$10 1934	30.00	60.00
$10 1934A	35.00	125

	F	XF
$10 1934 yellow seal	3,200	9,000
$10 1934A yellow seal	320	400
$10 1934B	160	350
$10 1934C	20.00	50.00
$10 1934D	30.00	40.00
$10 1953	30.00	75.00
$10 1953A	40.00	125
$10 1953B	25.00	75.00

Federal Reserve notes

The Federal Reserve System was created in 1913. It consists of 12 Federal Reserve banks governed in part by the U.S. government through the Federal Reserve Board, whose members are appointed by the president and confirmed by the Senate. Each of the Federal Reserve banks is composed of various member banks.

The paper money used today in the United States is issued by the Federal Reserve banks. Originally, Federal Reserve notes could be redeemed for gold. That changed in 1934.

Like all other U.S. paper money, Federal Reserve notes were reduced in size with Series 1928, in 1929.

Since 1993, new anticounterfeiting innovations have been added to the notes. Micro printing was incorporated in the design and around the frame of the portrait. Also, a transparent strip bearing the value and "USA" was embedded in the paper. It can be seen only when the note is held up to a light and cannot be photocopied.

These improvements were precursors to the first major overhaul of U.S. paper money since the 1920s. Beginning with the $100 bill in 1996, more changes were made, including larger portraits to show more detail and more white space on the reverse so watermarks could be added to the paper. A watermark is an image pressed against the paper while the newly printed note is drying. Like the transparent printed strip, it can be seen only when the note is held up to a light.

Among the most ingenious high-tech safeguards on the new notes is color-shifting ink, which alters its color depending on the angle of the light hitting it. The green Treasury seal has been retained, but the old letter seal indicating the Federal Reserve bank of distribution was replaced by the Federal Reserve System seal. These innovations were added to the $20 and $50 notes with Series 1996 and the $5 and $10 notes with Series 1999. The $1 note was not scheduled to change.

Starting in 2003, additional steps were taken to prevent counterfeiting. The $5, $10, $20, and $50 notes received multicolored background designs. The changes are also slated for the $100 note.

Federal Reserve notes are produced at the Bureau of Engraving and Printing's main facility in Washington, D.C., and at its Western Currency Facility in Fort Worth, Texas. Notes produced at Fort Worth have a small "FW" mark in the lower right corner of the face.

Most Federal Reserve notes produced since the 1930s are collected only in high grade. Dealers may be unwilling to buy even scarce pieces if they are not crisp uncirculated. Star notes, which have a star instead of one of the numerals in their serial numbers, are popularly collected in this series but, again, must be crisp to be desirable. Recent issues command no premium; they are sold at face value plus a handling fee to cover the dealer's costs.

For Series of 1988A, 1993, and 1995 $1 Federal Reserve notes, the BEP experimented with web presses for printing the notes. On web presses, the paper is fed into the presses on rolls. Traditionally, paper money has been printed on sheet-fed presses. The web-press $1 Federal Reserve notes can be distinguished from the regular notes in two ways: (1) On the front of regularly printed notes, there is a small letter and number to the lower right of the Treasury seal indicating the plate number. On web-printed notes, there will be only a number with no letter preceding it. (2) On the back of regularly printed notes, the plate number appears to the lower right of the "E" in "One." On web-printed notes, the number appears above the "E" in "One."

LARGE SIZE

RED SEAL, SERIES OF 1914

	F	XF

$5 Abraham Lincoln 300 600

	F	XF

$10 Andrew Jackson 400 1,250

	F	XF

$20 Grover Cleveland 400 2,000

	F	XF

$50 Ulysses S. Grant 2,750 4,500

	F	XF

$100 Benjamin Franklin 1,750 3,750

BLUE SEAL, SERIES OF 1914

	F	XF

$5 Abraham Lincoln 60.00 150
$10 Andrew Jackson 85.00 250

	F	XF

$20 Grover Cleveland 215 400
$50 Ulysses S. Grant 200 700
$100 Benjamin Franklin 400 1,250

BLUE SEAL, SERIES OF 1918

	F	XF

$500 John Marshall 7,000 30,000

	F	XF

$1,000 Alexander Hamilton.. 10,000 20,000
$5,000 James Madison, *rare* ....
$10,000 Salmon P. Chase, *rare* ....

SMALL SIZE, GREEN SEAL

Denomination	Series	Front	Back
$1	1963	Washington	Great Seal
$2	1976	Jefferson	Declaration of Independence signing
$5	1928	Lincoln	Lincoln Memorial
$10	1928	Hamilton	Treasury Building
$20	1928	Jackson	White House
$50	1928	Grant	Capitol
$100	1928	Franklin	Independence Hall
$500	1928-1934A	McKinley	500
$1,000	1928-1934A	Cleveland	Inscription
$5,000	1928-1934B	Madison	5000
$10,000	1928-1934B	Chase	10,000

	XF	CU
$1 1963	3.00	6.00
$1 1963A	3.00	5.00
$1 1963B	3.00	9.00
$1 1969	2.00	7.00
$1 1969A	2.00	5.00
$1 1969B	2.00	5.00
$1 1969C	3.00	7.00
$1 1969D	2.00	7.00
$1 1974	2.00	5.00
$1 1977	2.00	6.00
$1 1977A	2.00	6.00
$1 1981	2.00	7.00
$1 1981A	2.00	6.00
$1 1985	—	6.00
$1 1988	2.00	9.00
$1 1988A	2.00	6.00

	XF	CU
$1 1988A web press	7.75	40.00
$1 1993	2.00	6.00
$1 1993 web press	6.00	15.00
$1 1995	—	4.00
$1 1995 FW	—	4.00
$1 1995 web press	8.00	17.00
$1 1999	—	3.00
$1 1999 FW	—	3.00
$1 2001	—	3.00
$1 2001 FW	—	3.00
$1 2003	—	3.00
$1 2003 FW	—	3.00
$1 2003A	—	3.00
$1 2003A FW	—	3.00
$1 2006	—	3.00
$1 2006 FW	—	3.00
$1 2009	—	3.00
$1 2009 FW	—	3.00

	XF	CU
$2 1976	3.00	10.00
$2 1995	4.00	9.00
$2 2003 FW	—	9.00
$2 2003A FW	—	8.00

	F	XF
$5 1928	20.00	100

	F	XF
$5 1928A	15.00	75.00
$5 1928B	12.00	25.00
$5 1928C	500	1,500
$5 1928D	750	2,500
$5 1934	10.00	20.00

	F	XF
$5 1934 "Hawaii"	75.00	200
$5 1934A	10.00	20.00
$5 1934B	10.00	20.00
$5 1934C	10.00	20.00
$5 1934D	10.00	20.00
$5 1950	8.00	12.00
$5 1950A	10.00	18.00
$5 1950B	10.00	20.00
$5 1950C	8.00	10.00
$5 1950D	8.00	10.00
$5 1950E	15.00	25.00
$5 1963	8.00	10.00
$5 1963A	8.00	10.00
$5 1969	6.00	7.00
$5 1969A	6.00	8.00
$5 1969B	10.00	30.00

	XF	CU
$5 1969C	7.00	20.00
$5 1974	7.00	15.00
$5 1977	7.00	15.00
$5 1977A	10.00	35.00
$5 1981	8.00	25.00
$5 1981A	15.00	30.00
$5 1985	7.00	15.00
$5 1988	7.00	15.00
$5 1988A	7.00	15.00
$5 1988A FW	7.00	15.00
$5 1993	7.00	15.00
$5 1993	7.00	15.00
$5 1995	6.00	10.00
$5 1995 FW	—	10.00
$5 1999	6.00	10.00
$5 1999 FW	6.00	10.00
$5 2001	7.00	15.00
$5 2003	7.00	15.00
$5 2003 FW	7.00	15.00
$5 2003A FW	7.00	15.00
$5 2006 FW	7.00	15.00
$5 2006 FW colorized	7.00	15.00

	F	XF
$10 1928	35.00	125
$10 1928A	35.00	60.00
$10 1928B	18.00	30.00
$10 1928C	65.00	225
$10 1934	15.00	40.00
$10 1934A	11.00	12.00

	F	XF
$10 1934A "Hawaii"	100	275
$10 1934B	13.00	25.00
$10 1934C	11.00	15.00
$10 1934D	11.00	20.00

	XF	CU
$10 1950	20.00	75.00
$10 1950A	30.00	70.00
$10 1950B	20.00	35.00
$10 1950C	30.00	50.00
$10 1950D	20.00	50.00
$10 1950E	55.00	125
$10 1963	15.00	50.00
$10 1963A	20.00	50.00
$10 1969	15.00	40.00
$10 1969A	15.00	45.00
$10 1969B	50.00	150
$10 1969C	20.00	40.00
$10 1974	15.00	35.00
$10 1977	15.00	35.00
$10 1977A	15.00	35.00
$10 1981	20.00	40.00
$10 1981A	20.00	40.00
$10 1985	20.00	35.00
$10 1988A	20.00	35.00
$10 1990	—	20.00
$10 1993	—	20.00
$10 1995	—	20.00
$10 1999	—	20.00
$10 1999 FW	—	20.00
$10 2001	—	20.00
$10 2001 FW	—	20.00
$10 2003	—	15.00

	XF	CU
$10 2003 FW	—	15.00
$10 2004A FW	—	15.00
$10 2006 FW	—	15.00
$10 2009 FW	—	15.00

	F	XF
$20 1928	50.00	125
$20 1928A	60.00	150
$20 1928B	30.00	50.00
$20 1928C	225	700
$20 1934	225	700

	F	XF
$20 1934 "Hawaii"	700	2,000
$20 1934A	25.00	35.00
$20 1934B	25.00	35.00
$20 1934C	25.00	40.00

	XF	CU
$20 1934D	30.00	95.00
$20 1950	35.00	70.00
$20 1950A	30.00	70.00
$20 1950B	30.00	60.00
$20 1950C	35.00	50.00
$20 1950D	35.00	75.00
$20 1950E	25.00	70.00
$20 1963	35.00	75.00
$20 1963A	30.00	60.00
$20 1969	30.00	60.00
$20 1969A	40.00	80.00
$20 1969B	100	200
$20 1969C	30.00	60.00
$20 1974	30.00	55.00
$20 1977	30.00	60.00
$20 1981	35.00	75.00
$20 1981A	30.00	60.00
$20 1985	25.00	50.00
$20 1988A	30.00	60.00
$20 1990	25.00	45.00
$20 1993	—	40.00
$20 1993 FW	—	40.00
$20 1995	—	45.00
$20 1995 FW	—	45.00
$20 1996	—	30.00
$20 1996 FW	—	30.00
$20 1999	—	30.00
$20 1999 FW	—	30.00
$20 2001	—	30.00
$20 2001 FW	—	30.00

	XF	CU
$20 2004	—	30.00
$20 2004 FW	—	30.00
$20 2004A	—	30.00

$20 2004A FW	—	30.00
$20 2006	—	30.00
$20 2006 FW	—	30.00
$20 2009	—	30.00
$20 2009 FW	—	30.00

	F	XF
$50 1928	100	250
$50 1928A	70.00	100
$50 1934	—	60.00
$50 1934A	75.00	125
$50 1934B	70.00	125
$50 1934C	75.00	110
$50 1934D	75.00	110
$50 1950	80.00	100
$50 1950A	75.00	100
$50 1950B	60.00	80.00
$50 1950C	50.00	70.00
$50 1950D	55.00	100
$50 1950E	100	150

	XF	CU
$50 1963A	75.00	80.00
$50 1969	60.00	100
$50 1969A	75.00	100
$50 1969B	700	1,000
$50 1969C	65.00	75.00
$50 1974	70.00	115
$50 1977	55.00	75.00
$50 1981	70.00	115
$50 1981A	75.00	100
$50 1985	60.00	75.00
$50 1988	60.00	150
$50 1990	—	75.00
$50 1993	—	70.00

	XF	CU
$50 1996	—	60.00
$50 2001	—	70.00

	XF	CU
$50 2004 FW	—	70.00
$50 2004A FW	—	70.00
$50 2006 FW	—	75.00
$50 2009 FW	—	75.00

	XF	CU
$100 1928	250	750
$100 1928A	200	350
$100 1934	130	200
$100 1934A	180	400
$100 1934B	300	450
$100 1934C	200	400
$100 1934D	350	500
$100 1950	200	400
$100 1950A	—	240
$100 1950B	185	200
$100 1950C	—	200

$100 1950D	—	200
$100 1950E	200	300
$100 1963A	—	150
$100 1969	—	140
$100 1969A	—	180
$100 1969C	—	150
$100 1974	—	135
$100 1977	—	130
$100 1981	—	140
$100 1981A	125	160
$100 1985	—	150
$100 1988	—	175
$100 1990	—	150
$100 1993	—	160
$100 1996	—	120
$100 1999	—	125
$100 2001	—	125
$100 2003	—	135
$100 2003A	—	125
$100 2006	—	125
$100 2006 FW	—	125
$100 2006A	—	125
$100 2009	—	—
$100 2009 FW	—	—

	F	XF
$500 1928	850	1,300
$500 1934	750	1,250
$500 1934A	750	1,150
$500 1934B *specimens only*		
$500 1934C *specimens only*		

	F	XF
$1,000 1928	1,600	2,000
$1,000 1934	1,500	2,000
$1,000 1934A	1,500	2,000
$1,000 1934C *specimens only*		
$5,000 1928	20,000	105,000

	F	XF
$5,000 1934	20,000	70,000
$5,000 1934A *rare*		
$5,000 1934B *rare*		
$10,000 1928	—	170,000

	F	XF
$10,000 1934	46,000	70,000
$10,000 1934A *specimens only*		
$10,000 1934B *none known*		

Federal Reserve bank notes

Federal Reserve bank notes were issued by the 12 Federal Reserve banks rather than nationally chartered private banks. They were legal tender but not a government obligation; the obligation to redeem was with the Federal Reserve banks, not the U.S. Treasury.

Large-size notes have a blue Treasury seal on them. Small-size Federal Reserve bank notes were actually emergency currency printed on notes originally intended to become regular Series 1929 national currency. They were issued in 1933 and have a brown Treasury seal.

The name of the issuing Federal Reserve bank is printed on the note in the same location as the issuing bank on a national bank note.

Star notes are scarce and command a significant premium.

LARGE SIZE

	F	XF

$1 1918 George Washington..110 200

	F	XF

$2 1918 Thomas Jefferson 250 800

	F	XF
$5 1915 Abraham Lincoln	400	700
$5 1918 same	375	650

	F	XF
$10 1915 Andrew Jackson	1,100	4,000
$10 1918 same	1,250	5,000
$20 1915 Grover Cleveland	2,000	11,000
$20 1918 same	2,250	6,000
$50 1918 Ulysses S. Grant	10,000	17,500

SMALL SIZE, BROWN SEAL

	F	XF
$5 Boston	25.00	60.00
$5 New York	20.00	50.00
$5 Philadelphia	20.00	75.00
$5 Cleveland	20.00	50.00
$5 Atlanta	35.00	50.00
$5 Chicago	20.00	50.00
$5 St. Louis	500	1,500
$5 Minneapolis	40.00	300
$5 Kansas City	75.00	150
$5 Dallas	55.00	75.00
$5 San Francisco	1,000	10,000

	F	XF
$10 Boston	30.00	75.00
$10 New York	100	140
$10 Philadelphia	20.00	65.00
$10 Cleveland	20.00	100
$10 Richmond	25.00	100
$10 Atlanta	20.00	75.00
$10 Chicago	30.00	70.00
$10 St. Louis	20.00	60.00
$10 Minneapolis	25.00	75.00
$10 Kansas City	25.00	50.00
$10 Dallas	300	750
$10 San Francisco	75.00	150

	F	XF
$20 Boston	30.00	75.00
$20 New York	35.00	50.00
$20 Philadelphia	35.00	110
$20 Cleveland	30.00	70.00
$20 Richmond	30.00	175
$20 Atlanta	35.00	150
$20 Chicago	30.00	60.00
$20 St. Louis	30.00	100
$20 Minneapolis	30.00	100
$20 Kansas City	35.00	50.00
$20 Dallas	175	900
$20 San Francisco	100	135

	F	XF
$50 New York	75.00	150
$50 Cleveland	475	625
$50 Chicago	85.00	150
$50 Minneapolis	65.00	185
$50 Kansas City	75.00	160
$50 Dallas	1,000	2,000
$50 San Francisco	75.00	150

	F	XF
$100 New York	130	165
$100 Cleveland	125	150
$100 Richmond	150	300
$100 Chicago	125	150
$100 Minneapolis	150	175
$100 Kansas City	125	190
$100 Dallas	300	350

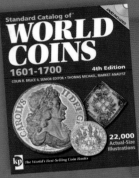
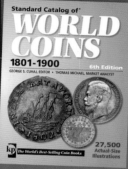
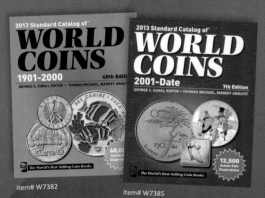